New Directions for
Child and Adolescent
Development

W9-AZH-747

Reed W. Larson
Lene Arnett Jensen
EDITORS-IN-CHIEF

William Damon
FOUNDING EDITOR

Beyond the Family: Contexts of Immigrant Children's Development

Hirokazu Yoshikawa
Niobe Way
EDITORS

Number 121 • Fall 2008
Jossey-Bass
San Francisco

BEYOND THE FAMILY: CONTEXTS OF IMMIGRANT CHILDREN'S
DEVELOPMENT
Hirokazu Yoshikawa, Niobe Way (eds.)
New Directions for Child and Adolescent Development, no. 121
Reed W. Larson, Lene Arnett Jensen, Editors-in-Chief

Microfilm copies of issues and articles are available in 16mm and 35mm,
as well as microfiche in 105mm, through University Microfilms, Inc.,
300 North Zeeb Road, Ann Arbor, Michigan 48106-1346.

ISSN 1520-3247   electronic ISSN 1534-8687

NEW DIRECTIONS FOR CHILD AND ADOLESCENT DEVELOPMENT is part of The
Jossey-Bass Education Series and is published quarterly by Wiley Sub-
scription Services, Inc., a Wiley company, at Jossey-Bass, 989 Market
Street, San Francisco, California 94103-1741. Periodicals postage paid at
San Francisco, California, and at additional mailing offices. Postmaster:
Send address changes to New Directions for Child and Adolescent Devel-
opment, Jossey-Bass, 989 Market Street, San Francisco, CA 94103-1741.

New Directions for Child and Adolescent Development is indexed in Cam-
bridge Scientific Abstracts (CSA/CIG), CHID: Combined Health Infor-
mation Database (NIH), Contents Pages in Education (T&F), Current
Abstracts (EBSCO), Educational Research Abstracts Online (T&F),
ERIC Database (Education Resources Information Center), Index
Medicus/MEDLINE/PubMed (NLM), Linguistics & Language Behavior
Abstracts (CSA/CIG), Psychological Abstracts/PsycINFO (APA), Social
Services Abstracts (CSA/CIG), SocINDEX (EBSCO), and Sociological
Abstracts (CSA/CIG).

SUBSCRIPTION rates: For the U.S., $85 for individuals and $280 for institutions. Please see ordering information page at end of journal.

EDITORIAL CORRESPONDENCE should be e-mailed to the editors-in-chief:
Reed W. Larson (larsonr@uiuc.edu) and Lene Arnett Jensen (ljensen@
clarku.edu).

Jossey-Bass Web address: www.josseybass.com

CONTENTS

1

From Peers to Policy: How Broader Social Contexts Influence the Adaptation of Children and Youth in Immigrant Families

Hirokazu Yoshikawa, Niobe Way

Abstract

*This chapter provides an overview of nonfamily contexts that shape the devel-
opment and adjustment of children and youth from immigrant families. It also
describes the four chapters in this special issue that focus on peer, network, legal,
and institutional contexts that influence the lives of immigrant parents and their
children. Directions for future research on the social contexts of development in
immigrant families are discussed.* © 2008 Wiley Periodicals, Inc.

NEW DIRECTIONS FOR CHILD AND ADOLESCENT DEVELOPMENT, no. 121, Fall 2008   © Wiley Periodicals, Inc.
Published online in Wiley InterScience (www.interscience.wiley.com) • DOI: 10.1002/cd.219

1

Immigration in the United States has become a central focus of policy and public concern in the first decade of the 21st century. Conundrums and questions with deep roots in U.S. history—such as the balance between inclusion and exclusion, state and federal responsibility, and whether certain groups are net benefits or drains on society—are being rehashed with regard to immigrant groups (Ellwood, 1988; Massey, 2003; S.1348, 2007). Lost in this debate for the most part is the question of how immigrant children and youth are faring. Although children of immigrant parents of some ethnic groups are doing quite well relative to their U.S.-born counterparts, some are not (Glick & Hohmann-Marriott, 2007; Kao, 1999; Schwartz & Stiefel, 2006; Suárez-Orozco, Suárez-Orozco, & Todorova, 2008). Research has provided some insight into the processes that explain such variation (Duran & Weffer, 1992; Portes & Rumbaut, 2001; Suárez-Orozco & Suárez-Orozco, 2001). However, such research has focused almost exclusively on family contexts, demographic and human capital characteristics, and school contexts. Portes and Rumbaut's influential segmented assimilation theory points towards characteristics of host communities, governments, and communities as influences on patterns such as downward and upward assimilation. However, the majority of studies explaining these patterns focus on the family and school as influences on developmental trajectories of children and youth in immigrant families. Few researchers have examined other contexts, such as peers, adult social networks, legal status, and institutions in relationship to developmental outcomes. These contexts have been posited as important in segmented assimilation and other theories of immigrant adaptation, but rarely instantiated in developmental research.

This special issue presents research studies that focus on the influence of peers, extended family networks, and legal and policy contexts on immigrant parents and their children. The studies focus on particular immigrant groups, including those from China, Mexico, the Dominican Republic, and elsewhere. Very different patterns are found across these immigrant groups, underscoring the importance of distinguishing among groups within pan-ethnic categories such as Latinos. The studies in this special issue also use a variety of methodologies including qualitative (in-depth case studies, semistructured interviews, ethnography) and quantitative methods (surveys analyzed using a variety of multivariate methods). Research on immigrant families can benefit greatly from mixing quantitative and qualitative methods (see Yoshikawa, Weisner, Kalil, & Way, 2008). Finally, the studies in this volume are conducted by scholars from psychology, public policy, and sociology. Thus, the exploration of immigrant parents and children is not limited by the methodological or conceptual constraints of any one discipline.

The Contexts of Development

The family is clearly a dominant socializing context for children in immigrant families. Families are the locus for decisions concerning whether to migrate, the primary source of support for navigating transitions, and the site for transmission of culturally based beliefs and practices to the children. Family factors, such as levels of parental education, language use, parenting practices, family structure, and parent involvement in school, help explain differences by generation of immigration and across immigrant groups in children's academic and cognitive outcomes (Fuligni, Tseng, & Lam, 1999; Han, 2006; Kao & Tienda, 1993; Nord & Griffin, 1999; Portes & Rumbaut, 2001). In addition, recent research has documented culturally specific socialization practices that appear to predict academic and socioemotional outcomes for particular immigrant groups (Caplan, Choy, & Whitmore, 1991; Chao, 2001; Conchas, 2001; Waters, 2001). However, family structures and processes do not fully explain differences in educational or social outcomes across generations or immigrant groups, or variation within groups, suggesting that other contextual influences are important as well.

Peer contexts as well as adult social networks are also likely to be important for immigrant children and youth. Such youth frequently spend as much time, if not more, with their peers and with extended family members and other adults. Thus, these contexts may influence immigrant youth as much as the immediate context of families. Other critical contexts for immigrant children and youth include more distal contexts (termed "macrosystems"; see Bronfenbrenner & Morris, 1998) such as legal, institutional, and policy contexts. These types of contexts, which are further removed from the daily lives of youth than the more proximal contexts of peers and adult social networks, offer numerous opportunities and impose various constraints in the lives of immigrant children and youth. They may influence children and youth through intervening changes in peer, school, neighborhood, and family settings (Yoshikawa & Hsueh, 2001). Thus, they too are likely to have a significant influence on immigrant children and youth. This special issue explores the ways in which both proximal and distal contexts influence the lives of immigrant parents and their children's cognitive and socioemotional development.

Proximal Contexts. Among the sets of contexts that are most immediate to the child are the peer and the extended family contexts. Peers greatly shape the social, emotional, and cognitive development of all children (Bukowski & Mesa, 2007) and may be particularly important in the case of immigrant children because it is often the reception of peers that determine the extent to which such children thrive. The extended family in the host and home countries, likewise, often serve as a critical support network for immigrant youth and likely influence the levels of adjustment of such youth. Yet very few researchers have examined such contexts among immigrant families. The existing research on peers has focused predominantly on nonimmigrant, White youth (Way, Gingold, Rotenberg, & Kuriakose, 2005), whereas the existing research on extended families has focused predominantly on nonimmigrant African American families. Two studies in this special issue focus on these critical contexts for immigrant

NEW DIRECTIONS FOR CHILD AND ADOLESCENT DEVELOPMENT • DOI: 10.1002/cd

parents and their children. Qin, Way, and Rana (pp. 27–42) use longitudinal data from two qualitative studies of Chinese immigrant families, to investigate the peer context. They focus on the reasons for the high levels of peer discrimination that are often experienced by Chinese immigrant youth (Qin, Way, & Mukherjee, 2008; Rosenbloom & Way, 2004). Their data reveal that various factors including beliefs about academic ability, immigrant status, language barriers, and physical appearance contribute to the high levels of ethnic/racial discrimination by nonimmigrant peers reported by Chinese immigrant youth. Such negative peer experiences pose a serious impediment to the ability of Chinese immigrant youth to thrive in the social and emotional domains. Their work draws attention to the importance of the peer context for the adjustment of immigrant youth.

In addition to the peer context, the extended family network is also important as it typically reinforces the beliefs and practices valued by the parents at home. Examining how this extended family network provides information, assistance, protection, advice, and support is critical for a more comprehensive understanding of the influence of these networks on the adjustment of immigrant youth. Using a sample of low-income Chinese immigrant families, Jin Li and her colleagues (pp. 9–25) investigate how families build social networks and how these networks function to support immigrant Chinese children's learning. Their findings suggest that families use a range of techniques (e.g., role models, siblings as comparisons) to help support their children's learning. For example, the authors find that families often identify an "anchor helper," a person sufficiently familiar with American schools, to guide the child's school learning by providing tutoring and academic advice. This study underscores the creative strategies families are using to support the academic adjustment of their children. It also extends theories of family processes in immigrant life beyond the typical notions of extended family size and social capital, to the specific functions that extended family members play in the socialization of children.

The research on proximal contexts in this issue underscores the importance of examining the role of nonfamily relationships as well as the extended family in the development of children in immigrant families. The studies reveal the ways in which both peers and adult social networks play an important role in the daily lives of children and adolescents from immigrant families and can be both supportive and challenging to their adaptation process. They extend hypotheses about the role of social networks and social capital in the literature on immigrant adaptation to pinpoint the specific ways in which networks influence youth learning and psychological well-being.

Distal Contexts. Broader social contexts, such as legal, institutional, and policy contexts, have also only begun to be studied relative to child and adolescent development. Although many studies have examined social class (indicators of socioeconomic status, such as parental education, income, and employment) as a source of variation in the trajectories of immigrant children and youth, few have examined the legal, institutional, or policy factors that may influence both family socioeconomic status and other family processes. The many studies that do exist on legal, institutional, and policy contexts related to immigration rarely incorporate data on parents or children (Borjas, 2001; Massey, 2003).

Two studies in this issue—Kalil and Chen's chapter and Yoshikawa, Godfrey, and Rivera's chapter—address the consequences of undocumented status for family life and child development. These studies find that undocumented parents (particularly Latina) experience higher levels of hardship and social exclusion. The study by Kalil and Chen examines whether legal status in immigrant families is related to food insecurity (the inability to buy the food one would want for one's family). The authors, utilizing one of the only large-scale longitudinal data sets in the country that ask parents about their citizenship status, find that parents who are both foreign-born and without legal status report higher food insecurity, in analyses controlling for a wide range of socioeconomic factors. In contrast, having a parent that is foreign-born with legal status is related to lower food insecurity, even when compared to children of native-born parents. In addition, they find that certain correlates of undocumented status—being Latino, having a larger household size, and lower levels of maternal education—partially explain the difference between citizen and noncitizen levels of food insecurity. These data suggest that children growing up in families with undocumented parents may be at nutritional risk, especially given the fact that these families are not eligible for the federal Food Stamp program. As one of the first studies to link legal to nutritional status among immigrant children, this study contributes to theory and evidence concerning citizenship status and children's health.

In their chapter, Yoshikawa, Godfrey, and Rivera utilize data from a longitudinal birth cohort study of infants born to immigrant Mexican and Dominican mothers, as well as to U.S.-born African American mothers. Data from other studies of New York City suggest that low-income parents from Mexico include a higher proportion of undocumented individuals than their counterparts from the Dominican Republic (Smith, 2006). The authors investigate access to financial services and drivers' licenses as aspects of undocumented parents' social exclusion that may have consequences for family life and child development. The authors find the lowest levels of household-level access to these resources among the group that in New York City is most likely to be undocumented: Mexican mothers. Lack of access to these resources was found to be associated with economic hardship and psychological distress, and those factors, in turn, predicted lower levels of cognitive ability on a standardized assessment at 24 months of age.

Together these studies move beyond traditional indicators of socioeconomic disadvantage to pinpoint the specific risk to family life and children's development that undocumented status may represent. Most studies of disadvantage focus on a very small set of parental economic indicators (income, education, earnings, and occupational status). The current studies show that legal status may be an understudied but important additional indicator of disadvantage with consequences for children, even in the first 2 years of life. They also suggest the particular risk to family life and child development that Latino families with undocumented status may face. (However, neither study had a large proportion of undocumented parents from other regions of the world, such as Asia or Eastern Europe. Future research should provide more knowledge about the risks that undocumented parents and their children from such regions face.)

These studies strengthen theories of the development of immigrant children and youth by linking what occurs in the home to factors that are directly affected by public policy. Policies of inclusion and exclusion, which define who has access to the benefits of citizenship status, can influence children's development through proximal family processes, such as the ability to provide the food one would like for one's family; experiences of economic hardship; and parental psychological symptoms of depression and anxiety (Fuligni & Yoshikawa, 2004). The family thus continues to be a central context of development, but family processes appear to be influenced by more macro processes through the potent "marker" of legal status. Such information about the developmental consequences of social exclusion or inclusion can inform current policy debates, such as those concerning forms of identification for undocumented immigrants.

This issue concludes with an integrative chapter summarizing future directions for a contextually rich, interdisciplinary field of study for children and youth in immigrant families. This chapter, by Carola Suarez-Orozco and Avary Carhill, eloquently addresses several challenges facing the field. First, they point out the different "blinders" that particular disciplines have in their view of the adaptation of immigrant youth. For example, psychologists, who have come late to the study of immigration, have tended to ignore many aspects of sending and receiving contexts in favor of specifying family processes that predict adaptation. Second, they point out that many contexts remain to be studied in a way that links specifically to developmental trajectories. These include not only the relational, legal, and institutional contexts considered in this issue, but also neighborhood contexts.

In summary, the work presented in this issue provides examples of where we think the study of immigrant families is headed in coming years. By embedding the commonly studied context of families within other social contexts—whether those of proximal settings, such as peers, or those that shape such settings, such as legal or institutional contexts—all of the contributing authors aim to broaden our knowledge of the influences that shape the lives and trajectories of children in immigrant families.

References

Barr, M. S. (2004). Banking the poor. *Yale Journal on Regulation, 21,* 121–137.
Borjas, G. J. (2001). *Heaven's door: Immigration policy and the American economy.* Princeton, NJ: Princeton University Press.

Bronfenbrenner, U., & Morris, P. A. (1998). The ecology of developmental processes. In W. Damon & R. Lerner (Eds.), *Handbook of child psychology: Vol. 1. Theoretical models of human development* (pp. 993–1028). New York: Wiley.

Bukowski, W. M., & Mesa, L. M. S. (2007). The study of sex, gender, and relationships with peers: A full or empty experience? *Merrill-Palmer Quarterly, 53,* 507–519.

Caplan, N., Choy, M. H., & Whitmore, J. K. (1991). *Children of the boat people: A study of educational success.* Ann Arbor, MI: University of Michigan Press.

Chao, R. K. (2001). Extending research on the consequences of parenting style for Chinese Americans and European Americans. *Child Development, 72,* 1832–1843.

Comprehensive Immigration Reform Act of 2007, S.1348, 110th Cong (2007).

Conchas, G. Q. (2001). Structuring failure and success: Understanding the variability in Latino school engagement. *Harvard Educational Review, 71,* 475–504.

Duran, B. J., & Weffer, R. E. (1992). Immigrants' aspirations, high school process and academic outcomes. *American Educational Research Journal, 29,* 163–181.

Ellwood, D. T. (1988). *Poor support: Poverty and the American family.* New York: Basic Books.

Fuligni, A. J., Tseng, V., & Lam, M. (1999). Attitudes toward family obligations among American adolescents with Asian, Latin American, and European backgrounds. *Child Development, 70,* 1030–1044.

Fuligni, A. J., & Yoshikawa, H. (2004). Investments in children among immigrant families. In A. Kalil & T. DeLeire (Eds.), *Family investments in children's potential: Resources and behaviors that promote success* (pp. 139–162). Mahwah, NJ: Erlbaum.

Glick, J. E., & Hohmann-Marriott, B. (2007). Academic performance of young children in immigrant families: The significance of race, ethnicity, and national origins. *International Migration Review, 41,* 371–402.

Han, W. (2006). Academic achievements of children in immigrant families. Manuscript under review.

Kao, G. (1999). Psychological well-being and educational achievement among immigrant youth. In D. J. Hernandez (Ed.), *Children of immigrants: Health, adjustment, and public assistance* (pp. 410–477). Washington, DC: National Academy Press.

Kao, G., & Tienda, M. (1993). Optimism and achievement: The educational performance of immigrant youth. *Social Science Quarterly, 76,* 1–19.

Levitt, P., & Waters, M. (2002). (Eds.). *The changing face of home: The transnational lives of the second generation.* New York: Russell Sage Foundation.

Louie, V. S. (2001). Parents' aspirations and investment: The role of social class in the educational experiences of 1.5- and second-generation Chinese Americans. *Harvard Educational Review, 71,* 438–474.

Louie, V. S. (2004). *Compelled to excel: Immigration, education and opportunity among Chinese Americans.* Palo Alto, CA: Stanford University Press.

Massey, D. (2003). *Beyond smoke and mirrors: Mexican immigration in an era of economic integration.* New York: Russell Sage Foundation.

Nord, C. W., & Griffin, J. A. (1999). Educational profiles of 3- to 8-year-old children of immigrants. In D. J. Hernandez (Ed.), *Children of immigrants: Health, adjustment, and public assistance* (pp. 348–409). Washington, DC: National Academy Press.

Portes, A., & Rumbaut, R. (2001). *Legacies: The story of the immigrant second generation.* Berkeley: University of California Press.

Qin, D., Way, N., & Mukherjee, P. (2008). The other side of the model minority story: The familial and peer challenges faced by Chinese American adolescents. *Youth and Society, 39,* 480–506.

Rosenbloom, S. R., & Way, N. (2004). Experiences of discrimination among African American, Asian American, and Latino adolescents in an urban high school. *Youth and Society, 35,* 420–451.

Schwartz, A., & Stiefel, L. (2006). Is there a nativity gap? Achievement of New York City elementary and middle school immigrant students. *Education Finance and Policy, 1,* 17–49.

Smith, R. C. (2006). *Mexican New York: Transnational lives of new immigrants.* Berkeley, CA: University of California Press.

Suárez-Orozco, C. S., & Suárez-Orozco, M. (2001). *Children of immigration.* Cambridge, MA: Harvard University Press.

Suárez-Orozco, C. S., Suárez-Orozco, M., & Todorova, I. (2008). *Learning a new land: Immigrant students in American society.* Cambridge, MA: Harvard University Press.

Waters, M. (2001). *Black identities: West Indian immigrant dreams and American realities.* Cambridge, MA: Harvard University Press.

Yoshikawa, H., & Hsueh, J. (2001). Child development and public policy: Towards a dynamic systems perspective. *Child Development, 72,* 1887–1903.

Yoshikawa, H., Weisner, T. S., Kalil, A., & Way, N. (2008). Mixing qualitative and quantitative research methods in developmental science: Uses and methodological choices. *Developmental Psychology, 44,* 344–354.

HIROKAZU YOSHIKAWA is a professor of education at the Harvard Graduate School of Education, Cambridge, MA.

NIOBE WAY is a professor of applied psychology at New York University's Steinhardt School of Culture, Education and Development, New York, NY.

Li, J., Holloway, S D., Bempechat, J., & Loh, E. (2008). Building and using a social network: Nurture for low-income Chinese American adolescents' learning. In H. Yoshikawa & N. Way (Eds.), Beyond the family: Contexts of immigrant children's development. *New Directions for Child and Adolescent Development, 121*, 9–25.

2

Building and Using a Social Network: Nurture for Low-Income Chinese American Adolescents' Learning

Jin Li, Susan D. Holloway, Janine Bempechat, Elaine Loh

Abstract

Little research has examined how low-income Asian American children are supported to achieve well in school. The authors used the notion of social capital to study higher versus lower achieving Chinese adolescents from low-income backgrounds. They found that families of higher-achieving adolescents built and used more effectively three kinds of social networks in lieu of direct parental involvement: (a) designating a helper in and outside the home for the child, (b) identifying peer models for the child to emulate, and (c) involving extended kin to guide the child jointly. These forms of social capital reflect Chinese cultural values applied to the challenges of immigrant adaptation. © 2008 Wiley Periodicals, Inc.

NEW DIRECTIONS FOR CHILD AND ADOLESCENT DEVELOPMENT, no. 121, Fall 2008 © Wiley Periodicals, Inc.
Published online in Wiley InterScience (www.interscience.wiley.com) • DOI: 10.1002/cd.220

Few people would doubt the essential role the family plays in child development. For a long time, however, the notion of family was considered no more than a collection of family members, extended kin, and the socioeconomic resources that they possess. Developmental researchers focused on the caregiver's direct interactions and his or her relationship with the child. Certainly, much can be gained in studying such micro processes within the family. However, in recent decades sociologists have introduced the concept of social capital to understand the often invisible, but powerful resources that families garner to support child development (Bourdieu, 1985; Coleman, 1988). Social capital includes people the family knows and information, assistance, protection, advice, and support such networks provide to the family. Indeed, researchers have shown that social capital is significant in predicting positive child outcomes (O'Brien, Murray, & O'Campo, 2006), particularly with regard to educational achievement (Lareau, 2000).

Research on social capital has essentially shifted the focus on the traditional notion of family to broader social contexts. Although such research remains scarce in child development, progress has been made (Lin, 2001; Portes, 1998). Research on how different social classes generate and use social networks has particularly enlightened our understanding. For example, middle-class families have a different structure of social networks from their working-class and poor counterparts. Middle-class families enroll their children in significantly more organized activities through which they connect to other parents. They also know many more professionals, and importantly, they know how to garner their support for dealing with school problems, curricular disputes, and placement of their children. Working-class and poor families rely on their kin as a source of support. However, they mostly use such support for daily survival and non-school-related social interactions. As a result, their social networks do not benefit their children's education in the same way as the networks built and used by middle-class families (Horvat, Weininger, & Lareau, 2003). As Stanton-Salazar (1997) further sums up, middle-class social capital is used to maximize individual access to mainstream economic gain, but working-class and poor people use their networks to respond to scarcity and conservation of resources.

One population for which social contexts are of particular relevance is immigrant families (IFs) who raise children in a different country. More than 60% of the current IFs consist of parents born outside but with children born inside the United States (U.S. Census Bureau, 2004). The process of childrearing in this context is vastly different from the one by which the parents themselves were raised. Many IFs are also from ethnic minority and low-income backgrounds. Yet, a puzzling phenomenon about children of IFs has been noted: Despite the extraordinary challenges they face, many children seem to beat the odds and achieve well in school (Suárez-Orozco & Suárez-Orozco, 2001). It begs the question as to how IFs provide support for their children. Focusing on how they build and use social networks in supporting their children's learning may yield important understanding.

What factors may influence how a given group of IFs build and use their networks? Previous research on nonimmigrant populations suggests that social class is a key factor (e.g., Horvat et al., 2003). We propose that socioeconomic status (SES) alone may not be sufficient in explaining network building and functions; there may be other important factors beyond the SES of IFs. Cultural values and orientations may also be an important source of variation among groups. Previous research has consistently documented the role culture plays in children's learning as well as related parental socialization (Hess & Azuma, 1991; Stevenson & Stigler, 1992). For example, Asian students more strongly believe in effort as a cause for achievement whereas European American, British, and Australian children believe more in ability as the cause (Walkins & Biggs, 1996). Thus, there may be unexplored interactions between social class and culture that have yet to be understood in what kinds of networks IFs feel they need and how they use them. Given that cultural values and orientations (culture hereafter for convenience) shape family relationships and forms of resource allocation (Leung & Bond, 1984), the kinds of networks families build and use may vary by culture (e.g., Koreans in Korea vs. Indians in India) and ethnicity (e.g., Korean Americans vs. Mexican Americans) in conjunction with social class (e.g., middle-class vs. low-income Korean Americans in the United States).

Thus, in the present article we focus on the interaction between social class and culture by examining a particular ethnic group: low-income Chinese families and their networks. We suggest, based on our data and analysis, that Chinese low-income families create and use a form of network that suits their need to foster their children's school learning. One essential factor underlies these Chinese families' networks and related deployment: living the mandate of their cultural learning model in the face of their harsh life struggles and challenges of immigrant adaptation. We present three particular strategies: family designated helpers, role models, and kin's involvement.

In what follows, we discuss first the Chinese cultural learning model as a family mandate and how this mandate is understood by Chinese families based on earlier research (Cheng, 1996; Lee, 1996; Li, 2001; Li & Wang, 2004; Zhou & Kim, 2006). Then we describe our research procedure and summarize some key findings. Whenever possible, we draw on research documenting middle-class Chinese immigrant families as an example to highlight low-income families' strategies. We conclude this article with suggestions for future research.

Chinese Learning Model as a Cultural Mandate

The Chinese learning model is profoundly influenced by Confucian teaching. Confucius' long-lasting influence lies in his fundamental teaching of the concept of *ren,* that is, a lifelong striving for any human being to become the most genuine, sincere, and humane person he or she can become. This concern of Confucius is not academic, not mind-oriented (as in the West), but moral in nature. The process of becoming *ren* is also called self-perfection by Confucius, who believed that human perfectibility can be sought by anyone. Those who commit themselves to the process of *ren* are called *junzi*. This outline of life purposes and its learning process is deeply inspiring to the Chinese because it is not only for everyone, but is also under each individual's control. *Junzi* is a human ideal in Chinese culture (Ames & Rosemont, 1999; de Bary, 1991; Li, 2003a).

According to Confucianism, those who have recognizable achievement along this moral/social path shall serve community and government, which is called *meritorious service* (Lee, 1996). This model of learning assumed such central importance that it became institutionalized during the 7th century with the Civil Service Examination system (Lee, 1985). As such, scholars of all backgrounds (who studied Confucian texts), not nobility alone, were selected as court officials. This system lasted over 12 centuries until its abolishment early in the 20th century. This unprecedented coalescence among moral achievement, academic learning, political power, social status, and economic gain led to the supremacy of learning in Chinese culture. Such learning (moral self-cultivation in the center along with intellectual development) has become cemented as an unquestionable and nonnegotiable value; therefore, this "moral mandate" has been transmitted from generation to generation. This learning model has tremendous motivational impact on Chinese people. The broadened curriculum and increased demands of modern education only intensify this value for the Chinese. Put in a different way, if one wants to be a good person, to be competent, to have power and status, to acquire wealth, one must learn; and if one wishes for all of these things, one must learn even more. In this value system, a person lacking pure intellectual achievement is unfortunate, but a person lacking morals is unacceptable (Cheng, 1996). In Chinese people's minds, achieving such learning brings honor, respect, and everything good in life. This is what is behind the statement that "education is the only means to a good life" that is so commonly echoed by most Chinese people. It is therefore not surprising to hear the poignant expression in present-day China: "Students are not allowed to fail, but only allowed to succeed" (只准成功，不准失败), as population growth escalates and competition for scarce resources becomes ever more fierce.

Beyond the value itself, the Chinese learning model specifies a set of learning virtues believed to be important personal dispositions that children must develop to learn well. They include determination, diligence, endurance of hardship, perseverance, concentration, and humility. Quiet, dedicated, contemplative learning is emphasized over fun and verbal expression. The best learner, therefore, is not one who merely uses his or her mind to inquire about the world (Li, 2003b), but one who applies himself or herself to study with these virtues (Li, 2002). Moreover, achievement is attributed to these personal virtues, and not learning well is attributed to a lack of these virtues. Recent research documents these learning virtues and styles as still pervasive among Chinese learners (Li, 2006).

Family Under the Cultural Mandate

Because ensuring good learning of their children as outlined earlier is an essential task for parents, Chinese families are organized to reach this goal. An important childrearing model that Confucianism also espouses rests on two basic, mutually constitutive, obligations: (a) parents' total commitment to children's welfare, and (b) children's reciprocal commitment to their parents known as *filial piety*. At the core of children's welfare is their learning, as discussed previously. Thus, the fulfillment of parental obligation is primarily gauged by how well their children learn and achieve in school (Zhou & Kim, 2006). Parents, in turn, make great efforts to instill the learning virtues in their children. Such daily effort to nurture children in their learning is a major component of their parental obligation understood as parental sacrifice, which can take many forms. For the non-poor families, it could be giving up a personal pleasure to take one's child to an enrichment program of music lessons. For poor families, it means enduring hardships (e.g., working several low-paying jobs to send one's child to weekend Chinese school). At the core of children's filial piety is honoring their parents' sacrifice by accomplishing what the sacrifice intends to serve—academic achievement. This dual obligatory principle is morally commanding and is understood by both parents and children (increasingly in age) as nonquestionable and nonnegotiable. In Chinese societies, upholding and practicing this principle is reason for respect, honor, and admiration from the community, school, and society. Research confirms that this basic learning model continues to operate in Chinese people across the world (Chao, 1996; Parmar, Harkness, & Super, 2004; Zhou & Kim, 2006).

This learning model propels families to build social networks from which they draw support. Often a kin member who has achieved well in school will become the role model of the entire kin and serve as the family guide for the young. Exemplary students also extend beyond the kin and become the role models of the entire town or village. They are invited by families and schools to share with other children how to work in school and how to give back to the community. Beyond the kin, parents consult friends, coworkers, and friends' friends on learning materials, opportunities, school selection, and other related socialization strategies. Families routinely enroll their children in existing weekend schools and community centers to provide extra learning where they meet other parents who, in turn, serve as further networks.

Immigrant Chinese Families. Although Chinese immigrants (CI) have been settling in the United States for more than a century, different waves of immigrants are distinct in important ways. Whereas early CIs were mostly laborers with little education and wealth, recent CIs tend to be highly educated with some even possessing a great deal of wealth. Instead of settling in the traditional ethnic enclaves such as Chinatown, new CIs move to suburbs and the newly termed *ethnoburbs* (with no single dominant ethnic group, an increasingly common residential phenomenon; Zhou & Kim, 2006). Nevertheless, the traditional CIs from low-income and low-education backgrounds continue to live in ethnic enclaves (although some groups are also scattered, e.g., Fujianese) mainly because the housing is more affordable, and the jobs there require few English skills (for example, Chinese grocery stores). Thus, the current Chinese immigrant trend seems to show two clear SES groups: middle-class and low-income. Whereas relatively more research exists on middle-class families, very little research has been done on low-income Chinese families.

To be sure, regardless of SES, CIs face the dual process of maintaining their own cultural values and adapting to new life in America. This process is rife with struggles and challenges. These difficulties range from language barriers, discrimination, segregation, stereotypes, and negative feedback from the mainstream culture about them (Rosenbloom & Way, 2004; Suárez-Orozco & Suárez-Orozco, 2001). As stated earlier, because of the dominant value of education for Chinese people, CIs may experience more, not less, family obligation and involvement in ensuring their children's learning (Zhou & Kim, 2006).

Because most parents already have some ideas about social networking strategies from their cultural tradition, they also build similar networks in their host country. For example, as Zhou and Kim (2006) documented, many Chinese middle-class families enroll their children in weekend Chinese schools. They socialize with other parents where information about U.S. schooling, learning materials, opportunities, and adaptive strategies is exchanged. However, it is not clear how low-income parents build networks because they have to work longer hours, often several jobs to provide necessities for their families. They may not have time or sophisticated knowledge to build similar networks as their middle-class peers. They may not have the resources to enroll their children in and take them to attend enrichment programs. As a result, low-income families may face more difficulties.

Our study therefore focused on how low-income CI families respond to and cope with the changes and challenges of the dual process of home socialization while adapting to American life. We targeted high school students because Chinese American adolescents are more likely to encounter conflicts at home and school (Wu & Chao, 2005). What we present is a portion of a larger study investigating home and school life among ethnic minority youth. Three research questions guided our current analyses: (1) What kind of parental involvement was there in their children's schooling? (2) How did families build social networks and how did these networks function to support their children's learning? (3) Were there differences in (1) and (2) between higher versus lower achieving students with this immigrant group?

If so, what were these differences? This analytical focus on high- versus low-achieving students within the same ethnic, but low-income, group can shed important light on the adaptive strategies (and by implication the lack thereof) that these families use to achieve their childrearing goals.

Method and Procedure

To study low-income CIs, we chose to base our study in Quincy, a midsized suburban city near Boston, Massachusetts, with a population of 88,000. Quincy's Chinese population was 10.8% (U.S. Census Bureau, 2004), the highest in the state (compared to the statewide population: 1.41%), mainly because of its proximity to Chinatown (1/2-hour subway ride). This city has a mixture of middle-class and working-class European and Asian Americans with few other minority groups. Half of the city's high school students (1,400) attended Harrison High School (half attend another high school; all names of schools and participants are pseudonyms). However, Harrison High School had a larger Asian American population than the town's overall percentage (30%). Approximately 13% of the school population was eligible for free/reduced price lunch.

We obtained permission from the school to contact low-income CI students who qualified for free/reduced price lunch. We recruited 32 self-identified Chinese ninth-grade students, half boys and half girls, most of whom were born in the United States with parents born abroad from Guangdong, China, Hong Kong (two families), and Fiji (one family). A few students had been born abroad, but had come to the United States during their elementary school years. All of them were proficient in English.

We interviewed each student twice using a standardized open-ended format. We asked initial questions, probed to clarify ambiguous meanings, elicit illustrative examples, and follow emergent issues. The data discussed in this article were obtained during the first interview, in which we asked the students to share their parents' information, their daily routines, detailing school learning, peer interactions, and family support for schoolwork at home. We also collected student grade point average (GPA) as an indicator of their achievement.

The interviews were audiotaped and transcribed verbatim. We used a qualitative data analysis software package to code themes pertaining to our research questions as well as constructs that emerged in our multistep process of reading the transcripts. We established 14 codes that were relevant to the central topic of the present article: (1) value of education, (2) value of hard work, if parents (3) asked about and (4) check the child's homework, (5) knew the child's classes, (6) discussed the child's electives, (7) knew the teachers, (8) attends school information meetings and (9) school activities, (10) contacted school about the child, (11) volunteered at school, (12) had nonschool person(s) to help the child, (13) used role models, and (14) had extended kin who helped. Intercoder reliability for the codes variables was computed with a sub-sample of 20 interviews, resulting in 70% to 100%, with an average of 87%.

Summary of Results

In the first three sections below, we summarize family demographic information to show that the parents and kin had limited education and resources to provide direct support to their children. Then in the following four sections, we present three forms of network building and its use by the family to compensate for what they lacked.

Sample Description. Most parents (78%) had a high school education or lower; five mothers had some tertiary education, but several had no schooling. Most fathers and some mothers had paid employment. The majority worked at low-paying jobs, including cook, waiter, dishwasher, administrative assistant, custodian, shelf stocker, and nursing home aide. A few owned small restaurants, which required them to work particularly long hours.

However, all but one child lived with two parents. Other than parents, most children also lived with other nonparent adults such as grandparents and aunts and uncles (average of 1.65 per family) as well as siblings and cousins. More than two thirds had extended families. However, many did not live in the same household, but resided either in the same town or in adjacent towns. Interaction among extended families was frequent and fluid. Some families came to each other's homes every day; others visited on a weekly basis. They dined together and helped each other with household chores, and cousins came in and out during the evening and weekends. All but three of the students spoke Chinese to their parents at home.

Student Achievement. The average grade point average (GPA) for these low-income students was 3.27 with a range of 4.23 to 2.09; 21 (66%) students had above a 3.0 GPA and 11 (34%) below it. Yet, regardless of their achievement level, 95% of the children indicated that education was the highest value to their families. Education was seen as the only way to a good life, conveying a clear sense that learning is nonquestionable and nonnegotiable to them. The only path to successful learning was, as 78% of the students revealed, to work hard. If that did not lead to the desired results, then the child needed to work harder. Even for highly achieving students, their parents encouraged them to be even better, as the highest achieving student, Karen, shared: ". . . if you're number 1, she [my mom] wants you to be even better than number 1 [meaning continuous self-improvement regardless of achievement]." These findings confirmed previous research done on middle-class families (Li, 2003b), thus providing support for our prediction that the cultural mandate holds true for both middle- and low-income families. Our hypothesis was further confirmed that immigration to the United States does not decrease the cultural mandate and familial willingness to carry the mandate out (Li, 2005).

NEW DIRECTIONS FOR CHILD AND ADOLESCENT DEVELOPMENT • DOI: 10.1002/cd

Parental Involvement. Despite these students' relative high achievement, there was, surprisingly, little direct parental involvement (in contrast to the findings about typical middle-class families). We examined two sets of indicators, one showing home involvement and the other school involvement. Both the higher and lower achieving students had a similar pattern of direct parental involvement. On average, only about a quarter of these families asked for or checked their children's homework or consulted on their electives in school. The only knowledge that these parents seemed to have was which classes their children took (similar in both groups at 87.5%, which was likely due to the fact that parents had to sign the school form to allow their children to take various classes). Regarding direct school involvement, less than 5% of parents did anything in these categories. In several categories, there was no involvement at all. The overwhelming reason for their lack of involvement was that they had no time because of their work schedules and that they did not know enough English to help with their children's homework or to communicate with school personnel. It is clear that these children's relatively impressive achievement, particularly the higher achievement, did not result from parental direct involvement.

To be sure, most students acknowledged that they needed academic help at some point—no matter how highly achieving they were. The question then remains who supported their learning if not the parents? Our analysis led to three possible family support strategies in building and using networks that may account, at least in part, for these children's achievement at school. Below we present these findings.

1. Anchor Helper Designated by the Family. Although parents were unable to provide direct academic help to their children, the family identified and designated at least one person in the home or extended family to be charged with guiding the child's school learning, providing tutoring and academic advice. This person, sufficiently knowledgeable about American school and dependable for support, we call an *anchor helper*. He or she, typically an older sibling or other relative, sometimes attended the same school but in a higher grade or was in college or had a professional career. As high as 86% of the higher achieving, but also 45% of the lower achieving students had such an anchor helper (see Table 2.1). Half of these anchor helpers for higher achieving but none for low-achieving students were from outside the immediate family (suggesting the higher achieving group perhaps used a larger network). A good example was offered by Ben whose college attending brother helped him with his school project: ". . . usually he gives me some pointers about stuff . . . , he read one of my research projects, and he said, well, Ben, this really sucks. So he gave me like this research book, and . . . it helped me a lot."

A girl's cousin, a senior in the same school, came to her home to play sports, but also to help her with her homework. Yet another boy tolerated his elementary school-aged sister who "got the habit" of pulling out unfinished

Table 2.1. Proportion of Network Strategies Among Low-Income Chinese Immigrant Families of High School Students by Achievement Level (N = 32)

Variable	Higher Achievers (N = 21)%	Lower Achievers (N = 11)%
Anchor helper	85.67	45.45
Use of role models	89.91	63.64
Kin support	55.50	18.18

homework sheets from his schoolbag to show them to their "clueless" parents. As a result, the boy made sure that he finished his homework so that his sister wouldn't find anything to report. This little sister's "butting in" behavior could only work when parents accepted, if not overtly enlisted, her help. The boy was likely to be fully aware of this monitoring style. When asked if he minded his sister's checking up on him, this boy only remarked light-heartedly, "I don't really care cause I usually get my homework done, so she doesn't find anything." These otherwise not-involved people acted in accordance with the cultural mandate of learning even when the primary caregivers were unable to meet this obligation themselves.

It is important to point out that this family function is regarded as network building and utilization because the anchor helper's charge is not regarded as sheer drainage of his or her personal energy, time, and financial resources. Rather, it is part of the reciprocal, mutual, but also emotionally laden support that Chinese families give to each other, a spirit that Rosemont and Ames (in press) retranslate into "family reverence." As such, the helper may be honored, take pleasure, and/or feel pride to be asked to serve this role. He or she may be quite willing to fulfill this family obligation and enjoy the family trust. In turn, this person's children may receive similar gratitude from those whom he or she has helped. This family network style of fulfilling mutual obligation may explain why a sense of family obligation has been found to predict Chinese American children's school achievement (Fuligni, 1997).

2. Role Models. A second form of networks is parents' frequent talking to their children's friends and learning about who among their peers did better at school. These good learning models include relatives, children of co-workers, and otherwise acknowledged good students in the community. Once parents discovered such models, they referred their own children to them often, in clear comparative terms, urging their children to emulate these models. If the better student was a sibling, then parents encouraged the other children at home to emulate the sibling. Overall, 77% of the children (see Table 2.1) said that their parents cited such models and wanted them to be like the models. In fact, more parents of higher achievers (90%) used models (compared to 64% of lower achievers). The predominant reason reported by the students was that the parents tried to motivate the children to strive to do better.

Some children found parents' pointing to the models annoying because they were made aware of the discrepancy between what their parents desired for them to achieve and what grades they brought home. However, the majority generally agreed with their parents that they needed to work harder to achieve better grades because they shared their parents' ultimate goal of getting a good education. To other students, counter-intuitively knowing that relatives of the same age and peers did better than them actually motivated them to work harder. The effect of using such a model is vividly illustrated by Jerry, a high-achieving student, when his parents compared him with his better-achieving sister:

> "She [sister] gets A's, and I get B's. If I fail a test, like I just did, and I'm like, oh why didn't I study? I just keep on thinking that over and over. . . . It's [parents' comparing him to his sister] annoying, but I am not mad at my sister. It gets me more annoyed when my parents are mad, cause, well, I should be annoyed at myself, too. I am not trying hard enough."

Ken, another higher achieving boy, recounted his mother's model use and how that also motivated him to work harder:

> . . . my mother, she likes to brag about me for some reason, and then she . . . sees someone else's report card for some reason . . . , and then she's like, look at this kid, she got all A's. And look at you, you got one B . . . , you're supposed to have more A's. And I'm like, isn't that enough? . . . Well, I wouldn't say demoralize, I would say that it would motivate me a little bit more . . . to work harder.

This way of using models has a long tradition in Chinese culture as discussed previously. All great scholars and learning models throughout Chinese history continue to live in oral tales, with many noted in the village records, the town's public monuments, and school curriculum (Wilson, 1980). Communities still take great pride in having high-achieving students. In 2005, the first author saw banners hanging across the roads and streets of her hometown in China, proudly announcing the top students in that year's college entrance examination. These learning models are readily available in communities, schools, and possibly kin systems. On her 2005 visit, the first author examined the Chinese-language curriculum for China's nine-year compulsory education program, which is still largely centralized in China, and found that 36% of the learning material contained these learner models. In America, Chinese-language newspapers also routinely print the profiles of winners of national, state, and local scholastic competitions (Zhou & Kim, 2006). They are free for parents to identify and to use, and they can be quite effective.

The purpose is to set exemplars within the community for children to emulate, not to put children down. This modeling accomplishes several goals. First, it sets clear achievement standards and benchmarks for children. Second, the standards and benchmarks are embodied in real human beings, not abstract, general, and frequently dry legal language as they are customarily done in governmental policies such as state achievement standards. Children can identify themselves with and to strive to be like these individuals because these models are similar to the children themselves in age and, importantly, in life circumstances. Third, by pointing out where their children are in their learning now and where they could go further, parents express their confidence and belief in their children. If parents did not believe that their children could reach a level equal to the exemplar, they would not bother to urge their children to strive for it. This confidence can be strongly motivating to children. Finally, parents, particularly less-educated parents as those in our current study, have reduced access to models and images that come in print (such as books and newspapers) even in their native language, let alone in English. However, these live models in the community are handy and persuasive for parents who cannot possibly motivate their own children if they themselves do not understand and admire these models. Research has long documented the effects of role models (Bryant & Zimmerman, 2003) and the influence that parents' strong convictions have on their children (Harkness & Super, 1996).

The use of the exemplar is particularly effective in a culture that does not view human potential as more or less determined at birth. Research on EAs indicates that although preschool children view persons as malleable, older children view persons as having fixed trait-like qualities that may determine their actions and outcomes (Dweck, 2006; Nisbett, 2003; Ruble, Eisenberg, & Higgins, 1994). Parents' pointing out inadequacies in their children in comparison with other children may have negative consequences on their children (Li & Wang, 2004; Wheeler & Suls, 2005). Realizing one's inadequacies that are not under one's control can be very painful (Brickman & Bulman, 1977). Therefore, EA parents' desire to shield their children from such comparisons is understandable, although comparisons within the family are often made. In contrast, the Chinese do not typically hold a fixed entity view of persons (Wang, 2004). According to Confucian fundamental teaching, every person, regardless of born differences, is believed capable of learning and endlessly self-improving so long as the person sets his or her mind on learning. The job of parents is to cultivate children's learning virtues, to set standards, and to guide them along the learning path. Therefore, parents' use of role models is less likely to be perceived by children as a putdown or unkind, but caring and supporting, as the above examples illustrate. Although CI children may hear conflicting messages from the mainstream culture (e.g., persons have fixed traits) and may be confused about these messages, the children in our sample did not construe their parents' use of role models as hurting their feelings. This may explain why many still acknowledged that they needed to work harder to achieve better even though they were annoyed.

3. Kin's Co-parenting. A third network use characteristic of low-income CI families is to invite, elicit, and even demand and oblige extended family kin to "co-parent" their children's learning. This kind of co-parenting in Chinese culture, or to use Chao's term (1994), *guan*-ing, extends across towns, states, even continents. Such co-parenting is an expected family obligation in many Chinese communities, especially if one is more educated. Even when such persons live afar, their help is sought after. Whereas middle-class families may have less need to enlist their extended kin's co-parenting, low-income and less educated parents may come to depend on their kin's involvement.

The pull and push are mutually constituted and executed. Kin members do not need an official invitation to "step in" or to "lecture" the children. Nor do they feel that they should reject a request if they are, in fact, asked to step in. More often, this form of co-parenting proceeds with fluid interactions of relatives asking about the children's school or offering solicited or unsolicited advice to the children. Tim, a high-achieving boy, said that his grandmother and uncle who lived in a separate city always gave him advice: "Almost everyone [including grandma and uncle]. Uh, be good in school, don't do anything stupid, do all your homework."

We did not specifically probe extended kin's co-parenting. Instead, we asked if there was anyone in their family who would give them advice about or help them with schoolwork. As high as 56% of the higher achieving students (compared to only 18% of the lower achievers) spontaneously shared the involvement of their extended kin (see Table 2.1). An example from Don, a higher achieving student, illustrates the working of this network form: "everybody in my family, all my aunts and uncles and cousins, they're all like, if you try harder you'd be like a really smart person." This student continued to express affection for and gratitude toward these family members for taking a personal interest in his learning. Another girl, Kate, also a higher achieving student, related that her grandmother was a schoolteacher in China who was glad to help her with math in elementary school. The most striking example was given by Jerry, whose relatives were actively involved even though they lived on a different continent: "My grandparents call a lot; they always ask me how I'm doing in school . . . my entire family, I think they're the most concerned about grades, cause whenever they call, it's always about school. . . . They call twice a week from Australia."

This kind of involvement by the extended family may indeed provide much needed support for these low-income families' effort to nurture their children, particularly in the face of their added challenges of immigration and acculturation.

Families with Lesser Networks. The three strategies of building and using networks seem to function well in these low-income CI families.

However, a persistent network pattern regarding the higher versus lower achieving students also emerged. In all three forms, more of higher achieving students' families had anchor helpers, identified role models, and had extended kin involvement. Because the sample was small, we did not perform any statistical analysis to test these differences. Yet, the case can be readily made that in every category when there was a difference, the families of the lower achieving students had less of the network and less use of it. Even when these students reported the three strategies noted in this article, their descriptions tended generally to be skeletal, brief, with few details and positive affect, compared to their higher achieving peers.

Conclusion and Future Research Directions

Home support may be a key factor in children's school achievement (Hart & Risley, 1995). However, home support can come in different forms and styles that are influenced by values and orientations of the group, as well as the family's SES. Whereas low-income Mexican American children, for example, may be strongly supported by religious communities (Holloway, Bempechat, Li, Elliot, & Hufton, 2005), low-income Chinese immigrant children may be supported through the types of networks and extended kin as documented in this study. Direct parental authority in daily school routines may be limited, but their cultural learning model is still upheld. To fulfill their parental duty and express their love to their children, these families build and maintain a form of social capital and use it creatively to nurture their children. These network strategies may consist of an anchor helper as a surrogate for direct parental guidance (middle-class parents may provide direct tutoring to their children instead of relying on anchor helpers). Nevertheless, parental responsibility never completely recedes; parents express their concerns and identify role models (middle-class parents are more likely to draw on role models from print and from their own SES circles). At the same time, extended kin stand by, watch, and contribute (middle-class parents may seek advice from their kin, but they may not need the kin's direct involvement). Whenever the families succeed, children buy into the values and the styles of this joint endeavor with positive affect. In turn, they are motivated to work hard to achieve well in school. Whenever this delicate system breaks down, children evade and even reject the family. In turn, they feel isolated, confused, and unmotivated to strive (Sung, 1987).

Ever since its introduction by sociologists, social capital has drawn a great deal of research attention from many social sciences. Theorists continue to debate about the nature of social capital, but developmental and education researchers are more concerned about how parents form social networks and how specifically they use such networks in their childrearing. In this article, we offer a useful lens into the Chinese immigrant family network. We can further benefit, for example, from interviewing family members directly about how they enlist support. We can also collect data on how children perceive such support and how they respond to it, focusing on incidences of success as well as conflicts. Finally, we can conduct observational research on how families actually build networks and how they use them. This line of research should also be extended to other ethnic groups and cultures. Comparing different forms and styles can enrich our understanding of the detailed ways different groups foster their children's development. This knowledge is valuable to parents, educators, and policy makers to further support and encourage their efforts to promote children's learning in school.

References

Ames, R. T., & Rosemont, H. Jr. (1999). *The analects of Confucius: A philosophical translation.* New York: Ballantine.

Bourdieu, P. (1985). The forms of capital. In J. G. Richardson (Ed.), *Handbook of theory and research for the sociology of education* (pp. 241–258). Westport, CT: Greenwood Press.

Brickman, P., & Bulman, R. J. (1977). Pleasure and pain in social comparison. In J. M. Suls & R. L. Miller (Eds.), *Social comparison processes: Theoretical and empirical perspectives* (pp. 149–186). Washington, DC: Hemisphere.

Bryant, A. L., & Zimmerman, M. A. (2003). Role models and psychosocial outcomes among African American adolescents. *Journal of Adolescent Research, 18,* 36–67.

Chao, R. K. (1994). Beyond parental control and authoritarian parenting style: Understanding Chinese parenting through the cultural notion of training. *Child Development, 65,* 111–119.

Chao, R. K. (1996). Chinese and European American mothers' views about the role of parenting in children's school success. *Journal of Cross-Cultural Psychology, 27,* 403–423.

Cheng, K.-M. (1996). *The quality of primary education: A case study of Zhejiang Province, China.* Paris: International Institute for Educational Planning.

Coleman, J. S. (1988). Social capital in the creation of human capital. *American Journal of Sociology, 94*(Suppl), S95–S120.

de Bary, W. T. (1991). *Learning for one's self.* New York: Columbia University Press.

Dweck, C. S. (2006). *Mindset: The new psychology of success.* New York: Random House.

Fuligni, A. J. (1997). The academic achievement of adolescents from immigrant families: The roles of family background, attitudes, and behavior. *Child Development, 68,* 351–363.

Harkness, S., & Super, C. M. (Eds.). (1996). *Parents' cultural belief systems: Their origins, expressions, and consequences.* New York: Guilford Press.

Hart, B., & Risley, T. R. (1995). *Meaningful differences in the everyday experience of young American children.* Baltimore: Brookes.

Hess, R. D., & Azuma, M. (1991). Cultural support for schooling: Contrasts between Japan and the United States. *Educational Researcher, 20*(9), 2–8.

Holloway, S. D., Bempechat, J., Li, J., Elliot, J., & Hufton, N. (2005). Academic resilience in cultural context: What do high-achieving African American, Chinese American, and Mexican American students learn from their families? Unpublished manuscript, University of California–Berkeley, Berkeley, CA.

Horvat, E. M., Weininger, E. B., & Lareau, A. (2003). From social ties to social capital. *American Educational Research Journal, 40,* 319–351.

Lareau, A. (2000). *Home advantage: Social class and parental intervention in elementary education.* Lanham, MD: Rowman & Littlefield.

Lee, T. H. C. (1985). *Government education and examinations in Sung China, 960–1278.* Hong Kong: Chinese University Press.

Lee, W. O. (1996). The cultural context for Chinese learners: Conceptions of learning in the Confucian tradition. In D. A. Watkins & J. B. Biggs (Eds.), *The Chinese learner* (pp. 45–67). Hong Kong: Comparative Education Research Centre.

Leung, K., & Bond, M. H. (1984). The impact of cultural collectivism on reward allocation. *Journal of Personality and Social Psychology, 4,* 793–804.

Li, J. (2001). Chinese conceptualization of learning. *Ethos, 29,* 111–137.

Li, J. (2002). A cultural model of learning: Chinese "heart and mind for wanting to learn." *Journal of Cross-Cultural Psychology, 33,* 248–269.

Li, J. (2003a). The core of Confucian learning. *American Psychologist, 58,* 146–147.

Li, J. (2003b). U.S. and Chinese cultural beliefs about learning. *Journal of Educational Psychology, 95,* 258–267.

Li, J. (2005). Mind or virtue: Western and Chinese beliefs about learning. *Current Directions in Psychological Science, 14,* 190–194.

Li, J. (2006). Self in learning: Chinese adolescents' goals and sense of agency. *Child Development, 77,* 482–501.

Li, J., & Wang, Q. (2004). Perceptions of achievement and achieving peers in U.S. and Chinese kindergartners. *Social Development, 13,* 413–436.

Lin, N. (2001). Social capital: A theory of social structure and action. Cambridge, UK: Cambridge University Press.

Nisbett, R. E. (2003). *The geography of thought.* New York: Simon & Schuster.

O'Brien, C. M., Murray, N. S., & O'Campo, P. J. (2006). Neighborhood matters: Racial socialization of African American children. *Child Development, 77,* 1220–1236.

Parmar, P., Harkness, S., & Super, C. M. (2004). Asian and Euro-American parents' ethnotheories of play and learning: Effects on preschool children's home routines and school behaviour. *International Journal of Behavioral Development, 28,* 97–104.

Portes, A. (1998). Social capital: Its origins and applications in modern society. *American Review of Sociology, 24,* 1–24.

Rosemont, H. Jr., & Ames, R. T. (in press). *The classic of family reverence: A philosophical translation.*

Rosenbloom, S. R., & Way, N. (2004). Experiences of discrimination among African American, Asian American, and Latino adolescents in an urban high school. *Youth & Society, 35,* 420–451.

Ruble, D. N., Eisenberg, R., & Higgins, E. T. (1994). Developmental changes in achievement evaluations: Motivational implications of self-other differences. *Child Development, 65,* 1095–1110.

Stanton-Salazar, R. D. (1997). A social capital framework for understanding the socialization of racial minority children and youths. *Harvard Educational Review, 67,* 1–40.

Stevenson, H. W., & Stigler, J. W. (1992). *The learning gap.* New York: Simon & Schuster.

Suárez-Orozco, C., & Suárez-Orozco, M. (2001). *Children of immigration.* Cambridge, MA: Harvard University Press.

Sung, B. L. (1987). *The adjustment experience of Chinese immigrant children in New York City.* New York: Center for Migration Studies.

U.S. Census Bureau. (2004). *We the people: Asians in the United States, Census 2000 Special Report.* Washington, DC: Author.

Wang, Q. (2004). The emergence of cultural self-constructs: Autobiographical memory and self-description in European American and Chinese children. *Developmental Psychology, 40,* 3–15.

Watkins, D. A., & Biggs, J. B. (Eds.). (1996). *The Chinese learner: Cultural, psychological, and contextual influences.* Hong Kong: Comparative Education Research Centre.

Wheeler, L., & Suls, J. (2005). Social comparison and self-evaluations of competence. In A. J. Elliot & C. S. Dweck (Eds.), *Handbook of competence and motivation* (pp. 566–578). New York: Guilford Press.

Wilson, R. (1980). Conformity and deviance regarding moral rules in Chinese society: A socialization perspective. In A. Kleinman & T. Lin (Eds.), *Moral and abnormal behavior in Chinese culture* (pp. 117–136). Dordrecht, Netherlands: D. Reidel.

Wu, C.-X., & Chao, R. K. (2005). Intergenerational cultural conflicts in norms of parental warmth among Chinese American immigrants. *International Journal of Behavioral Development, 29*(6), 516–523.

Zhou, M., & Kim, S. S. (2006). Community forces, social capital, and educational achievement: The case of supplementary education in the Chinese and Korean immigrant communities. *Harvard Educational Review, 76*, 1–29.

JIN LI is an associate professor of education and human development in the Education Department, Brown University.

SUSAN D. HOLLOWAY is an adjunct professor, School of Education, University of California, Berkeley.

JANINE BEMPECHAT is an associate professor in the Department of Human Development, Wheelock College.

ELAINE LOH was a research assistant to the project and now lives in Los Angeles, California.

Qin, D. B., Way, N., & Rana, M. (2008). The "model minority" and their discontent: Examining peer discrimination and harassment of Chinese American immigrant youth. In H. Yoshikawa & N. Way (Eds.), Beyond the family: Contexts of immigrant children's development. *New Directions for Child and Adolescent Development, 121,* 27–42.

3

The "Model Minority" and Their Discontent: Examining Peer Discrimination and Harassment of Chinese American Immigrant Youth

Desiree Baolian Qin, Niobe Way, Meenal Rana

Abstract

Using an ecological framework, the authors explore the reasons for peer discrimination and harassment reported by many Chinese American youth. They draw on longitudinal data collected on 120 first- and second-generation Chinese American students from two studies conducted in Boston and New York. Our analyses suggested that reasons for these experiences of harassment lay with the beliefs about academic ability, the students' immigrant status and language barriers, within-group conflicts, and their physical appearance that made them different from other ethnic minority or majority students. Implications and future research are also discussed. © 2008 Wiley Periodicals, Inc.

The first author would like to thank her mentors Dr. Marcelo Suárez-Orozco and Dr. Carola Suárez-Orozco, co-directors of Immigration Studies at NYU, for their support of this research within the Longitudinal Immigrant Student Adaptation Study. The LISA study was supported by the Spencer Foundation, the William T. Grant Foundation, and the Ford Foundation. The second author gratefully acknowledges the support of the National Science Foundation and the William T. Grant Foundation for the work described in this chapter.

Eighteen-year-old Chen Tsu was waiting on a Brooklyn subway platform after school when four high school classmates approached him and demanded cash. He showed them his empty pockets, but they attacked him anyway, taking turns pummeling his face. He was scared and injured—bruised and swollen for several days— but hardly surprised. At his school, Lafayette High in Brooklyn, Chinese immigrant students like him are harassed and bullied so routinely that school officials in June agreed to a Department of Justice consent decree to curb alleged "severe and pervasive harassment directed at Asian-American students by their classmates." . . . Nationwide, Asian students say they're often beaten, threatened and called ethnic slurs by other young people, and school safety data suggest that the problem may be worsening. Youth advocates say these Asian teens, stereotyped as high-achieving students who rarely fight back, have for years borne the brunt of ethnic tension as Asian communities expand and neighborhoods become more racially diverse.

Associated Press, *November 14, 2005*

Racism has been part of the Asian American experience since the beginning of Asian American history. Despite considerable progress that Asian Americans have made in various domains, most notably in education, they continue to experience discrimination and unfair treatment (Young & Takeuchi, 1998). Recent research shows that Asian American youth consistently report higher levels of peer discrimination and harassment in and out of school than their non-Asian peers (Kohatsu et al., 2000; Qin, Way, & Mukherjee, 2008; Rosenbloom & Way, 2004; Way, Santos, Niwa, & Kim, in press). Negative peer experiences have detrimental effects on students' psychological and social well-being (Greene, Way, & Pahl, 2006). However, limited research to date has been conducted to examine why such high levels of peer discrimination and harassment happen to Asian American students. In this chapter, we draw from two qualitative studies conducted in Boston and New York to explore the reasons for these frequent reports of peer discrimination and harassment among Chinese American first- and second-generation youth. Findings from this study can help researchers and practitioners understand why peer discrimination happens and inform schools and other social agencies in their efforts to intervene and protect students from harassment and victimization.

Peer Context and Adolescent Development

The peer context is considered a critical ecological context in adolescent development (Bronfenbrenner, 1979). Developmental research has consistently documented that peer relations have a significant impact on adolescent psychological well-being (Jones, Newman, & Bautista, 2005). High-quality peer relations protect adolescents from social anxieties (La Greca & Harrison, 2005), enhance social competence and interpersonal sensitivity, and are linked to positive psychological adjustment (Greene et al., 2006; Way & Pahl, 2001). Negative peer relations (e.g., peer discrimination and victimization) has been found to be related to low self-esteem, depressive symptoms, and social anxiety in adolescents (Fisher, Wallace, & Fenton, 2000; Greene, Way, & Pahl, 2006; Gee, Spencer, Chen, & Takeuchi, 2007; La Greca & Harrison, 2005; Noh, Kaspa, & Wichrama, 2007; Storch & Masia-Warner, 2004). Recent studies conducted by Way and her research team suggest that peer discrimination based on race or ethnicity by non-Asian peers is a major challenge for many Asian American youth across the United States (e.g., Greene et al., 2006; Rosenbloom & Way, 2004). In one of their studies, peer ethnic/race discrimination, or the extent to which students experienced racial or ethnic discrimination by their peers was more influential in the prediction of psychological well-being than peer support (Greene et al., 2006).

Peer Discrimination and Harassment

A number of recent studies show that Asian American students report higher levels of ethnic/race-based peer discrimination than students from other minority groups (Alvarez, Juang, & Liang, 2006; Choi, Meininger, & Roberts, 2006; Fisher et al., 2000; Goto, Gee, & Takeuchi, 2002; Greene et al., 2006; Grossman & Liang, 2008; Kohatsu et al., 2000; Rivas, Hughes, & Way, in press; Rosenbloom & Way, 2004; Way et al., in press). Alvarez and colleagues' (2006) study of Asian American college students found that 98% reported experiencing at least one racial micro-aggression such as being treated rudely in the past year. Fisher and colleagues (2000) found that Chinese and Korean students reported higher levels of distress from peer discrimination than their African American, Hispanic, and White peers. More specifically, over 80% of Chinese and Korean American students reported being called names, and close to 50% reported being excluded from social activities or threatened as a result of their race. Rivas-Drake, Hughes, and Way (2008) found that Chinese American early adolescents reported higher levels of peer teasing and harassment than their African American peers. Similarly, Way and her colleagues found in their 4–5 year longitudinal study of discrimination among Black, Latino, and Asian American high school students that Chinese American youth from predominantly immigrant families reported the highest levels of peer discrimination. Further, they found that Chinese American students' levels of perceived peer discrimination remained consistently high through high school years (Greene et al., 2006; Way et al., in press). In addition, they found that African Americans and Latino Americans reported discrimination by their teachers and other adults, whereas the Chinese American youth reported physical as well as verbal harassment by their non-Asian peers (Rosenbloom & Way, 2004; Qin et al., 2008). These patterns were particularly salient for those Chinese

NEW DIRECTIONS FOR CHILD AND ADOLESCENT DEVELOPMENT • DOI: 10.1002/cd

Americans who were first-generation immigrants. Other studies have found that Asian Americans were frequently teased and bullied by non-Asian peers (e.g., Huang, 2000; Louie, 2004).

Drawing on Mead's symbolic interactionism framework, Grossman and Liang (2008) describe mechanisms through which an individual is influenced by the images mirrored back from others to the self through a process where these evaluative feedbacks are internalized in one's identity and sense of self-worth. Suárez-Orozco (2000) illustrates a similar process where "negative social mirroring" can lead an immigrant youth to develop negative self-perceptions. These negative self-perceptions, in turn, are likely to be associated with poor psychological adjustment outcomes (Alvarez & Helms, 2001). Adolescents are particularly attuned to external messages about themselves (Phinney, 2000). Indeed, research shows that experiences of discrimination and negative appraisals about one's ethnic group are often internalized in the adolescents' sense of self and may reduce feelings of control in adolescence and foster feelings of helplessness, frustration, and depressive moods over time (Greene et al., 2006). Among Asian American youths and adolescents, ethnic/race-based peer discrimination and harassment have been linked to increases in depression and declines in self-esteem (Alvarez & Helms, 2001; Green et al., 2006; Grossman & Liang, 2008; Lee, 2005; Qin et al., 2008; Rivas-Drake, Hughes, & Way, 2008).

Although research has documented high prevalence of peer discrimination experienced by Asian American youths and their negative impact on these students' psychological adjustment, few studies have closely examined why such high levels of discrimination happen in the first place to Asian American youths. Some scholars have pointed out that the underlying reasons for discrimination may be different for Asian Americans than African Americans (Fisher et al., 2000; Grossman & Liang, 2008). Although discrimination against African Americans may be related to competence, discrimination against Asians is more likely associated with their "perpetual foreigner" status (Cheryan & Morin, 2005). Examining why Asian American adolescents experience peer discrimination can help inform school-based intervention efforts that aim to protect students from perpetual harassment and victimization and improve their psychological and social adjustment. Drawing on qualitative in-depth data from two longitudinal studies of first- and second-generation Chinese American youth that took place from 1996 to 2001, our investigation aims to explore the reasons Chinese American youth from immigrant families report such high levels of peer discrimination and harassment. We focus on the experiences of Chinese adolescents from immigrant families for two reasons. First, Chinese Americans constitute one of the largest subgroups among Asian Americans. Second, research has shown that peer discrimination distress is particularly pronounced in Asian American youths, including Chinese American youth, from immigrant backgrounds (Qin et al., 2008; Tsai, 2006).

Method

Sample. Our sample consists of 120 adolescents from two qualitative studies of Chinese American students in public schools in metropolitan areas. One study was conducted in the Boston area and had a sample of 80 Chinese American students and the second study was conducted in New York City and had a sample of 40 Chinese American students. Of the participants, the great majority (88%) were first-generation immigrant students, born in China, Hong Kong, Taiwan, or Macau, and immigrated to the United States before age 10. The rest were second-generation immigrants, whose parents emigrated from mainland China. The adolescents in the study conducted in New York City were recruited from mainstream English classrooms and were fluent English speakers. The adolescents in the study conducted in Boston were recruited mostly from English as Second Language classrooms in urban schools. Some students (about 20%) were recruited from mainstream English classrooms in middle-class, mostly White neighborhoods. The sample was fairly balanced in terms of gender: 55% ($n = 66$) of the participants were girls and 45% were boys ($n = 54$). The average age of the adolescents was 13 years at the beginning of the study ($SD = 1.70$). Students in our sample came from mixed socioeconomic families. Roughly a quarter of the parents attained elementary education; a quarter of the parents attained middle or high school level education; and close to a quarter of the parents had some college or beyond college education. Overall, our sample was loosely representative of the Chinese American population in the United States, particularly in terms of education level. The large range in years of education and professional experiences in our sample was consistent with census data that Chinese immigrants were overrepresented at both high and low ends of the educational spectrum and form a bimodal distribution in terms of education (U.S. Census, 2003).

Procedure. The data for both studies were collected from 1996 to 2001 (the first study from 1997–2001 and the second study from 1996–000), using semistructured and structured interviews with Chinese American adolescents from immigrant families. Five annual interviews were conducted with students in the Boston study and in the New York study. A team of trained researchers, including the authors, conducted interviews with the adolescents. In the student interviews, we asked questions about peer relationships (e.g., "How would you describe your relationships with peers at school?"). Given the English fluency of most of the adolescents in the New York-based study (they were more likely to come from second-generation immigrant families), all the interviews with these adolescents were conducted in English. For the Boston-based study, the majority of the interviews were conducted in Mandarin or Cantonese in the first 3 years and more than a third of the interviews were conducted in English in the final 2 years of the study (others were conducted in Mandarin or Cantonese). All interviews conducted were taped and translated into English (if conducted in other languages).

NEW DIRECTIONS FOR CHILD AND ADOLESCENT DEVELOPMENT • DOI: 10.1002/cd

Data Analyses. We used a process of open coding (see Strauss & Corbin, 1990) to generate themes from the interview data from both studies. We first read each interview and created "narrative summaries" that condensed the interview material while retaining the essence of the stories being told by the adolescents (see Miller, 1991). Data analysts who looked for themes in the summaries read each narrative summary independently. A theme retained for further analysis had to be identified as a theme by at least two of the three authors independently, in any one year of the study. Once themes were generated and agreed upon, each data analyst returned to the original interviews and noted in what year in the project and where in the interview itself these themes emerged.

It is important to note that the findings presented below are limited by several methodological constraints. The sample was neither random nor representative. Our participants were first- or second-generation immigrant adolescents, all attending schools in urban areas in the northeastern United States. Some issues that we discuss, e.g., immigration status and language barriers, were salient issues for this groups of adolescents and were not likely to represent experiences of third-generation and beyond Chinese American adolescents. However, other issues related to physical size or the model minority perception may apply to a wider range of Chinese American students.

Results

Analyses of data show that more than half of students in our studies reported incidents of ethnic and racial tension and peer discrimination at school. The form of peer discrimination included physical harassment as well as verbal taunts and slurs. Students reported being "beaten," "bullied," "tripped," "hit," "pushed," "kicked," and "thrown things at" both inside the school (e.g., in the hallway, or in the bathroom) and outside (e.g., in a park, or on the school bus). For example, Lin, a 13-year-old girl, said, "I was beaten and bullied here in the U.S. . . . the Black and White students beat me and bullied me, like when I was in a park, they'd throw things at me for no reason . . . There are some Blacks here, and Whites as well, they bully us all the time."

Similarly, when asked what the most difficult thing was after migration, 16-year-old Carl who came from Hong Kong responded,

> The most difficult thing is being bullied by both Blacks and Whites. They bully Chinese and Vietnamese students. They walk by and push you deliberately. They use expletives . . . In Hong Kong, no one treats me like that . . . They are not targeting one individual student, they target the entire group of Chinese students.

Students also reported verbal harassment at schools, e.g., being "cursed," called racial slurs like "Chino," and "told to go back to China." For example, 13-year-old Lin talked about being called names by her non-Chinese peers at school, "They call us 'girls from the country.' They don't respect us . . . [It happens] sometimes at the hallways, sometimes in the homeroom." Michael, a 14-year-old boy, said about his non-Chinese peers at school: "They usually walk up to me [and go] 'Hey Chino.' They just insult me [and] my race."

Besides these visible and audible forms of harassment and bullying, students also reported more subtle, nonverbal forms of poor treatment by some of their peers such as being ignored, socially ostracized, or being given certain "disgusted" "bad looks," students occupying seats and not allowing Chinese students to sit, or students not wanting to sit next to Chinese students.

Factors Associated With Harassment and Discrimination by Peers. The peer discrimination and harassment experienced by Chinese American youth have been previously reported (Greene et al., 2006; Qin et al., 2008; Rosenbloom & Way, 2004; Way et al., in press). What is often missing from these accounts, however, is a more thorough understanding of why these acts of discrimination and harassment are so frequent. Our research suggests there are five factors that motivate much of the discrimination and harassment experienced by Chinese American youth: (1) immigration status and language issues; (2) the higher levels of academic achievement among some of the Chinese American students in comparison to their non-Chinese peers; (3) the perceived preference for the Chinese American students by the teachers in the school; (4) differences in physical size between Chinese American students and non-Asian students; and (5) lack of group solidarity among the Chinese American students. Some of these themes have been discussed previously (see Rosenbloom & Way, 2004; Way et al., in press).

Immigration Status and Language. Our analysis shows that first-generation immigrant students were the most likely to report verbal and physical bullying. During interviews, first-generation immigrant students talked about three main factors that often led to peer prejudice and bullying: (a) speaking Chinese; (b) their English accent; and (c) their immigrant status, i.e., being in bilingual classes.

For most first-generation Chinese American students who often relied on Chinese (e.g., Mandarin, Cantonese, or other dialects) for communication, speaking a different language was one thing that was often easily picked out by non-Chinese peers. For example, Sally, who had been in the United States for 6 years, described the situation when she first arrived: "When I was in sixth grade, people would always say that I was speaking Chinese with others. They would imitate what we said and laugh about it . . . They don't know anything [about China], yet they think what I do is strange."

Lack of English proficiency is another reason they got teased by their non-Chinese peers. For example, 16-year-old Tina remembered, "When I first came to the U.S., I did not speak that much English. Some people at school teased me, made fun of me, and spoke something in English that I did not understand." Chinese students also reported being teased for having accents or making mistakes while speaking English. Tommy said after

3 years of being in the U.S., "the most difficult thing is English. My English is still not as good as my classmates'. If I make a mistake while I'm talking, they laugh at me." Tommy and many other recently arrived Chinese students were often quite preoccupied with their lack of English proficiency, which was exacerbated by their native peers' language policing and teasing. In fact, May, a second-generation Chinese girl, stated that there was a stereotype of "typical Chinese can't speak good English" at her school:

> They call you "Chino" and stuff like that. And then even more, they think that typical Chinese can't speak good English . . . sometimes I get this feeling that, yeah, they'll be thinking, like . . . Chinese kids, they learn to speak English, they speak, you know, broken English or something like that, you know? So, they'll be making fun of you if you do.

Although the students often attributed the harassment to actual or perceived language barriers, language barriers are confounded with immigration status or being in bilingual classes so that those who were first-generation immigrants to the United States were more likely to feel harassed due to language barriers by peers. "We are bilingual, they are regular," was a common sentiment for many first-generation immigrant students who experienced tension and harassment at school.

Academic Achievement and Its Discontent. Another common factor that students cited for being bullied is related to the "model minority" stereotype. In interviews, about 15% of our respondents talked about being treated poorly or bullied for "getting good grades," "being too smart," being "geeks," "nerdy," "studying too much," and "not having fun." For example, 14-year-old Lillian talked about being ostracized socially by her non-Chinese peers: "Sometimes people in my school do not consider me as their friend. They sometimes say things that hurt my feelings, but they are not aware of it. For example, when I asked them what they were talking about, they said, 'none of your business.' Later on, when they did not understand the homework, they came to ask me. Maybe I am of a different race . . . or maybe I am more hardworking than them . . . they always say I study too much or do too much work." Academically Lillian felt validated because other students would come to her to get help; however, socially she felt isolated and shunned by her peers.

Students also talked about the resentment other students felt against the Chinese American students regarding academics. For example, Bobby said, "in school some Americans will bully Chinese and tease we're too smart." When asked to give advice to recently arrived immigrant students, Bobby said, "Expect what you wouldn't expect. Everything is different. The way people here do things. The way school is. So consider things before doing them, the effects, etc. For example, most Chinese kids are very smart and raise hands all the time. People think you are a nerd and you are showing off." The fear of being perceived as a "nerd" and the poor treatment from peers because of their "nerdy" image were discussed more often in the interviews by boys than by the girls. However, during interviews, some girls also mentioned resentment from peers because of their academic achievement. For example, Xue, shortly after arrival in her American school, related that "When I first came to the U.S., some students in my school asked me what nationality I was. I answered 'Chinese.' They then give me this disgusted look . . . they again asked 'why do you Chinese always have to do better than us?'" Resentment from other students toward the Chinese American students regarding their perceived academic skills was felt among the Black students as well. When asked if she had ever experienced discrimination, Sheerah, an African American student from a New York school that some of our Chinese participants attended, commented, "The teachers think that the Chinese kids can do everything."

Teachers' Preferences and Student Resentment. As discussed by Rosenbloom and Way (2004), our interview data indicated that it was often the teachers' explicit statements that "Chinese kids can do everything" that frustrated the non-Chinese kids more than the Chinese American students' actual academic achievement. In many classes, non-Chinese and Chinese students discussed the obvious preference that many of the teachers had for the Chinese American students and how both the Chinese and non-Chinese students thought it was unfair to the other students. A Chinese American boy in his sophomore year of high school discussed at great length the unjust treatment that the Black and Latino students received because of the teachers' high expectations for the Chinese American students and their lower expectations for "everyone else." There were, furthermore, numerous examples of teachers' making explicit statements to other students as well as to the researchers on the New York and Boston projects that they greatly preferred to teach the Chinese students. One English teacher the first author interviewed in a school of mainly African American, Latino, and Chinese students sang high praises of the Chinese students: "They are so hard-working and so respectful, always on time, just such a delight to work with! If they get me to teach students like this, I will never retire for the rest of my life!" These explicit preferences made many of the non-Chinese students quite frustrated and angry, and they vented their anger on the Chinese American students themselves.

On the one hand, the model minority myth may serve some Chinese American students well by encouraging the teachers to have high expectations of them; on the other hand, this myth haunted the Chinese kids as it led to other students, Black, Latino, and White, to resent and harass them for the preferential treatment they received from the teachers (see Rosenbloom & Way, 2004). This complex dynamic was evident across most of the schools in which we conducted our research.

Physical Attributes. Another reason for peer discrimination and harassment was related to physical size and strength. According to about 20% of our participants, Chinese American students, both first- and second-generation immigrant students, were often perceived as "small," "weak," "skinny," "nerdy," and easy targets for bullying. This is most pronounced in boys' experiences. For example, Qiang, a 14-year-old boy, said, "American people think all Chinese people are weak, they always bother Chinese people, always call them 'Chinos' and all this stuff, 'cuz they think that Chinese are like, all weak; that these Americans should beat the Chinese up—that's why they bother them." Similarly, 16-year-old boy Ming, who attended school with mostly Chinese, Latino, and Black peers, talked about peer bullying in his school by Black and Latino students: "they always picking on me; so I'm not sure it's 'cause I'm skinny or the glasses or something . . . that's why sometimes I don't like being Chinese 'cause they're small; they get picked on by these big Black and Spanish people." Thus for Ming and Qiang, peer bullying and teasing could at least partially be attributed to the perception of a lack in physical size, strength, both important signs of masculinity in schools.

Physical size and perceived weakness was a struggle that at its root is a struggle of masculinity for many Chinese American boys (Eng, 2001; Yoshikawa, Wilson, Chae, & Cheng, 2004; Wilson & Yoshikawa, 2004). Traditional Chinese culture places education, morality, self-cultivation, and gentleness in men as valued qualities (Sung, 1987). In the Chinese culture, physical strength is often contrasted negatively with mental or intellectual capacities. The Chinese idiom "strong limbs, simple mind" clearly shows the bias against physical size and strength. However, in the U.S. context, proving one's masculinity through activities involving physical strength such as sports is such an important part of male identity development that boys learn to wear the "masculine straightjacket" very early on (Pollack, 1998). The lack of emphasis on Western norms of masculinity within the Chinese American community (Eng, 2001) may lead to particularly high levels of teasing or bullying from peers at school.

"We don't stick together." A number of our students attributed the fact that Chinese "don't stick together" as one of the reasons they were so often the victims of discrimination and harassment. Many tensions among the Chinese American students based on immigrant status discouraged group solidarity among them. For example, Ting, a 15-year-old Chinese girl, talked about being teased by her Chinese peers because she did not speak English well:

> When I just came to United states because I am Chinese right and I don't understand English then my classmates, just like, teasing me, just like, "you don't know English, why you here?" . . . I don't understand. All the teasing—people who just like born in here like ABC [American-born Chinese]. I think they should not do that to me because the same thing is they are Chinese right? . . . and they are just like Americans.

Conflicts among immigrants from different regions of China have also emerged in recent years. In both New York and Boston, the within-group tension among Chinese students was primarily between the Cantonese and the Fujianese, people from two adjacent provinces in Southern China. The Fujianese are newcomers whereas the Cantonese have been in the United States for a longer period of time. Conflicts in concentrated urban areas have been noted in recent years as large number of Fujianese are perceived as "taking over" sections of the traditionally Cantonese territories in major urban Chinatowns in New York and Boston. The conflicts in the communities have also been felt in schools. Tian, a Fujianese girl living in Boston who had been in the United States for a number of years, observed in her school that when she first came a few years ago, she was the only Fujianese student in her class; however, now, "almost half the class is Fujianese." Tian talked about her efforts to help the newly arrived Fujianese students who often felt shunned by the Cantonese students because of regional and language differences: "[in the bilingual program,] because they speak Cantonese, and if you don't speak Cantonese, you will feel that they are strangers. They won't talk to you. They feel that it is not OK to befriend Fujianese people." Another student in New York expressed her perplexity around the tension between the Cantonese and the Fukenese:

> Even Chinese people tease Chinese people, I mean like Cantonese people and Fukenese Fujianese people. They don't get along with each other. I don't know, I mean, I could get along with anyone fine as long as they don't judge me, but I don't get what's the point of having Cantonese against Fukenese people and Fukenese people against Cantonese.

Conflicts resulting from generational (e.g., first vs. second generation), regional (e.g., Cantonse vs. Fujianese, or Hong Kong vs. Mainland China), linguistic (e.g., different Chinese dialects) differences within the Chinese American community are increasingly becoming salient as more diverse groups of Chinese are immigrating to the United States in recent years. As our findings suggest, the differences may also serve to divide the Chinese youth in schools, which also contribute to high levels of negative peer experiences.

The differences within the Chinese American community are particularly difficult for students because of the potential support that fellow Chinese peers could provide to deal with discrimination. For example, Bobby, who talked about Chinese students being teased and verbally bullied at school for being smart, had the following advice for students who experienced peer discrimination: "Talk to someone, their friends or someone else, if they face discrimination. But not talk to parents because they can't really help you that much—they don't really understand discrimination among kids which is more verbal." Indeed, very few students we interviewed indicated that they discussed these experiences with their parents. They usually resorted to fellow Chinese peers for support. When there is division among the Chinese peers, coping can be more difficult.

NEW DIRECTIONS FOR CHILD AND ADOLESCENT DEVELOPMENT • DOI: 10.1002/cd

Discussion

In this chapter, we explored the factors that perpetuate the high rates of discrimination reported by Chinese American first- and second-generation immigrant students. Our findings show that Chinese American immigrant students experienced high levels of verbal, physical, and nonverbal discrimination and harassment from non-Chinese peers, confirming previous research findings (Greene et al., 2006; Rosenbloom & Way, 2004). Our study contributes to the literature on peer bullying and discrimination by highlighting the multiple contributing factors that may be associated with peer harassment and discrimination for Chinese American youth, including immigration status and languages, the model minority perception, physical size, and conflicts within the Chinese American community. These experiences of harassment are likely to be a significant source of stress and have been found to be linked to poor psychological adjustment for Chinese American students, particularly during adolescence (Greene et al., 2006; Rosenbloom & Way, 2004).

Our findings point to important issues facing Chinese American students that have not been adequately addressed in current research and practice. First, academic achievement continues to be the focus of most research on Chinese and Asian American youth. A growing body of research suggests that these youth and particularly those from immigrant families are also experiencing remarkably high levels of depression (Centers for Disease Control, 1995, 1997, 2003), low-levels of self-esteem (Greene et al., 2006; Rhee, Chang, & Rhee, 2003; Way & Robinson, 2003), and poor social adjustment (Uba, 1994; Qin, 2008; Way & Chen, 2000; Way & Pahl, 2001). More research is needed to understand why this Asian American youth experience higher levels of psychosocial distress than expected, particularly in the context of their relatively high academic achievement. Second, as our findings demonstrate, the social and emotional toll of the "model minority" perception can be quite high for Chinese American youth. In the last two decades, research has been conducted to understand the ways in which the "model minority" myth ignores the diverse academic needs of Asian American students (see Lee, 1996). However, few studies have examined the ways in which this stereotype negatively influences the social worlds of Asian American students. As our findings demonstrate, the perception that Asian American students are smart and favored by teachers often leads to peer ostracism and resentment. It is important for future research to continue to examine how the model minority stereotype may negatively impact the social and psychological adjustment of Asian American students. Third, for Chinese American boys, the social toll of the "model minority" image may be even higher. The construction of masculinity is a deeply cultural process with important implications for social dynamics at school. On one hand, the lack of emphasis on aggression or physical toughness may help Chinese American boys in their educational success (Connell, 2000). On the other hand, this emphasis is in

NEW DIRECTIONS FOR CHILD AND ADOLESCENT DEVELOPMENT • DOI: 10.1002/cd

sharp contrast to the mainstream code of masculinity. Chinese American boys thus are likely to be easy targets in the other boys' efforts to prove their own masculinity (Qin, 2008; Suarez-Orozco & Qin-Hilliard, 2004). Finally, the diversity among the Chinese American students at school is likely to mirror the increasing diversity within the larger Chinese American community due to generation, regional, linguistic, and cultural differences. At most schools in the urban areas with a substantial Chinese American population, there is a lack of identity or cohesive force that can unify students to support each other, particularly when faced with peer bullying. Most of the research on Chinese American students has focused on the Cantonese-speaking students near Chinatown. The experiences and dynamics of the recent immigrants from Fujian province and some northern provinces and how these dynamics influence students' social relations at school should also be examined.

In the majority of cases of ethnic tension and harassment, the school authorities do an inadequate job of addressing these issues and protecting the victims. Quite often, schools choose to avoid dealing with these issues that are considered sensitive and troublesome. As Semons (1991) pointed out, "Negative comments about Asians were overheard in the presence of teachers, who did nothing to interrupt them. Students could therefore infer that prejudice against Asians was acceptable" (p. 147). It is important for teachers and other school personnel to be aware of how these dynamics may shape the experiences of Chinese American students at school. In particular, it would be helpful for schools to establish guidelines and direct interventions in curbing different forms of peer bullying, e.g., verbal and physical harassment. To stop the root of peer bullying, it is also important to establish a healthy school environment. This can be done at the classroom level by introducing students to different cultures with a positive light in social studies curricula. It can also be achieved through different organized activities and programs at school that aim specifically to promote cultural understanding and exchanges between students from different backgrounds. Maintaining a healthy school environment where students from different backgrounds can interact positively will promote the healthy development of all children, girls and boys, native and immigrant alike.

References

Alvarez, A. N., & Helms, J. E. (2001). Racial identity and reflected appraisal as influences on Asian American's racial adjustment. *Cultural and Diversity and Ethnic Minority Psychology, 7,* 217–231.

Alvarez, A. N., Juang, L., & Liang, C. T. (2006). Asian Americans and racism: When bad things happen to "model minorities." *Cultural and Diversity and Ethnic Minority Psychology, 12,* 477–492.

Asian Youths Suffer Harassment in Schools. (2005, November 15). The Associated Press, p. 1.

Bronfenbrenner, U. (1979). *The ecology of human development: Experiments by nature and design.* Cambridge, MA: Harvard University Press.

Centers for Disease Control and Prevention. (2003). *Youth Risk Behavior Survey.* Atlanta, GA: National Center for Chronic Disease Prevention and Health Promotion, Division of Adolescent and School Health.

Centers for Disease Control and Prevention/National Council for Health Statistics. (1995). *Health, United States 1994.* Hyattsville, MD: U.S. Public Health Service.

Centers for Disease Control and Prevention/National Council for Health Statistics. (1997). *Monthly Vital Statistics Report, 46*(1). Hyattsville, MD: U.S. Public Health Service.

Cheryan, S., & Morin, B. (2005). Where are you *really* from?: Asian Americans and identity denial. *Journal of Personality and Social Psychology, 89,* 717–730.

Choi, H., Meininger, J. C., & Roberts, R. E. (2006). Ethnic differences in adolescents' mental distress, social stress, and resources. *Adolescence, 41,* 263–283.

Connell, R. W. (2000). *Teaching boys: The men and the boys.* Berkeley, CA: University of California Press.

Eng, D. (2001). *Racial castration: Managing masculinity in Asian America.* Durham, NC: Duke University Press.

Fisher, C. B., Wallace, S. A., & Fenton, R. E. (2000). Discrimination distress during adolescence. *Journal of Youth & Adolescence, 29,* 679–695.

Gee, G. C., Spencer, M. S., Chen, J., & Takeuchi, D. (2007). A nationwide study of discrimination and chronic health conditions among Asian Americans. *American Journal of Public Health, 97,* 1275–1282.

Goto, S. G., Gee, G. C., & Takeuchi, D. T. (2002). Strangers still? The experience of discrimination among Chinese Americans. *Journal of Community Psychology, 30,* 212–224.

Greene, M., Way, N., & Pahl, K. (2006). Trajectories of perceived adult and peer discrimination among Black, Latino, and Asian American adolescents. *Developmental Psychology, 42,* 218–238.

Grossman, J. M., & Liang, B. (2008). Discrimination distress among Chinese American adolescents. *Journal of Youth and Adolescence, 37,* 1–11.

Huang, W. J. (2000). *The interaction between identity and schooling of Asian American high school students.* Unpublished doctoral dissertation, Ohio State University, Columbus, OH.

Jones, D. C., Newman, J. B., & Bautista, S. (2005). A three-factor model of teasing: The influence of friendship, gender, and topic on expected emotional reactions to teasing during early adolescence. *Social Development, 14,* 421–439.

Kohatsu, E. L., Dulay, M., Lam, C., Concepcion, W., Perez, P., Lopez, C., et al. (2000). Using racial identity theory to explore racial mistrust and interracial contact among Asian Americans. *Journal of Counseling and Development, 78,* 334–342.

La Greca, A. M., & Harrison, H. M. (2005). Adolescent peer relations, friendships, and romantic relationships: Do they predict social anxiety and depression? *Journal of Clinical Child & Adolescent Psychology, 34,* 49–61.

Lee, R. M. (2005). Resilience against discrimination: Ethnic identity and other-group orientation as protective factors for Korean Americans. *Journal of Counseling Psychology, 52,* 36–44.

Lee, S. (1996). *Unraveling the "model minority" stereotype: Listening to Asian American youth.* New York, NY: Teachers College Press.

Louie, V. (2004). *Compelled to excel: Immigration, education, and opportunities among Chinese Americans* (p. 225). Stanford, CA: Stanford University Press.

Miller, B. (1991). *Adolescents' relationships with their friends.* Unpublished doctoral dissertation, Harvard Graduate School of Education, Cambridge, MA.

Noh, S., Kaspa, V., & Wichrama, K. (2007). Overt and subtle racial discrimination and mental health: Preliminary findings for Korean immigrants. *American Journal of Public Health, 97,* 1269–1274.

Phinney, J. S. (2000). Identity formation across cultures: The interactions of personal, societal, and historical change. *Human Development, 43,* 27–31.

Pollack, W. (1998). *Real boys: Rescuing our sons from the myths of boyhood.* New York: Holt & Company.

Qin, D. B. (2008). Doing well vs. feeling well: Understanding family dynamics and the psychological adjustment of Chinese immigrant adolescents. *Journal of Youth and Adolescence, 37,* 22–35.

Qin, D. B. (2008). Being 'good' or being 'popular': Gendered and ethnic identity formation of Chinese Immigrant adolescents. *Journal of Adolescent Research.* Manuscript submitted for publication.

Qin, D. B., Way, N., & Mukherjee, P. (2008). The other side of the model minority story: The familial and peer challenges faced by Chinese American adolescents. *Youth and Society, 39,* 480–506.

Rhee, S., Chang, J., & Rhee, J. (2003). Acculturation, communication patterns, and self-esteem among Asian and Caucasian American adolescents. *Adolescence, 3,* 749–768.

Rivas, D., Hughes, D., & Way, N. (in press). Racial socialization and discrimination as predictors of ethnic identity among middle school students. *Journal of Research on Adolescence.*

Rivas-Drake, D., Hughes, D., & Way, N. (2008). A closer look at peer discrimination, ethnic identity, and psychological well-being among urban Chinese American sixth graders. *Journal of Adolescent Research, 37,* 12–21.

Rosenbloom, S. R., & Way, N. (2004). Experiences of discrimination among African American, Asian American and Latino Adolescents in an urban high school. *Youth and Society, 35,* 420–451.

Schoen, C., Davis, K., Collins, K. S., Greenberg, L., Des Roches, C., & Abrams, M. (1998). *The Commonwealth Fund Survey of the Health of Adolescent Girls.* New York: The Commonwealth Fund.

Semons, M. (1991). Ethnicity in the urban high school: A naturalistic study of student experiences. *Urban Review, 23,* 137–158.

Storch, E. A., & Masia-Warner, C. (2004). The relationship of peer victimization to social anxiety and loneliness in adolescent females. *Journal of Adolescence, 27,* 351–362.

Strauss, A., & Corbin, J. (1990). *Basics of qualitative research: Grounded theory procedures and techniques.* Newbury Park, CA: Sage.

Suarez-Orozco, C. (2000). Identities under siege: Immigration stress and social mirroring among the children of immigrants. In A. Robben & M. M. Suarez Orozco (Eds.), *Cultures under siege: Collective violence and trauma* (pp. 194–226). New York, NY: Cambridge University Press.

Suarez-Orozco, C., & Qin-Hilliard, D. B. (2004). The cultural psychology of academic engagement: Immigrant boys' experiences in U.S. schools. In N. Way & J. Chu (Eds.), *Adolescent boys.* New York: New York University Press.

Sung, B. L. (1987). *The adjustment experience of Chinese immigrant children in New York City.* New York: Center for Migration Studies.

Tsai, J. H. (2006). Xenophobia, ethnic community and immigrant friendship network formation. *Adolescence, 41,* 285–298.

Uba, L. (1994). *Asian Americans: Personality patterns, identity, and mental health.* New York: Hillsdale Press.

U.S. Census Bureau. (2003). *Profile of the foreign-born population in the United States.* Washington, DC: U.S. Department of Commerce.

Way, N., & Chen, L. (2000). Close and general friendship among African American, Latino, and Asian American adolescents from low-income families. *Journal of Adolescent Research, 15,* 274–301.

Way, N., & Pahl, K. (2001). The predictors of friendship quality among ethnic minority, low-income adolescents. *Journal of Research on Adolescence, 11,* 325–349.

Way, N., & Robinson, M. (2003). A longitudinal study of the effects of family, friends, and school experiences on the psychological adjustment of ethnic minority, low-SES adolescents. *Journal of Adolescent Research, 18,* 324–346.

Way, N., Santos, C., Niwa, E., & Kim, C. (in press). A contextualized understanding of ethnic identity among Chinese American, African American, Puerto Rican, and

Dominican youth. In M. Azmitia (Ed.), *The intersection of social and personal identities. New Directions for Child and Adolescent Development.*

Wilson, P. A., & Yoshikawa, H. (2004). Experiences of and responses to discrimination among Asian and Pacific Islander gay men. *AIDS Education and Prevention, 16*, 65–83.

Yoshikawa, H., Wilson, P. A., Chae, H. W., & Cheng, J. (2004). Do family and friendship networks protect against the effects of discrimination on mental health and HIV risk among Asian and Pacific Islander gay men? *AIDS Education and Prevention, 16*, 84–100.

Young, K., & Takeuchi, D. T. (1998). Racism. In L. C. Lee & N. W. S. Zane (Eds.), *Handbook of Asian American psychology* (pp. 401–432). Thousand Oaks, CA: Sage.

DESIREE BAOLIAN QIN is an assistant professor of human development in the Department of Family and Child Ecology at Michigan State University.

NIOBE WAY is a professor of applied psychology at New York University.

MEENAL RANA is a doctoral candidate in Child Development in the Department of Family and Child Ecology at Michigan State University.

NEW DIRECTIONS FOR CHILD AND ADOLESCENT DEVELOPMENT • DOI: 10.1002/cd

Kalil, A., & Chen, J-H. (2008). Mothers' citizenship status and household food insecurity among low-income children of immigrants. In H. Yoshikawa & N. Way (Eds.), Beyond the family: Contexts of immigrant children's development. *New Directions for Child and Adolescent Development, 121*, 43–62.

Mothers' Citizenship Status and Household Food Insecurity Among Low-Income Children of Immigrants

Ariel Kalil, Jen-Hao Chen

Abstract

Recent data have shown that children of immigrant noncitizens experience more persistent and higher levels of food insecurity than the children of citizens following welfare reform. However, little is known about the range of factors that might explain different rates of food insecurity in the different populations. In this study, the authors used national data from the Early Childhood Longitudinal Study–Kindergarten cohort to assess this question, using multivariate probit regression analyses in a low-income sample. They found that households of children (foreign and U.S.-born) with noncitizen mothers are at substantially greater risk of food insecurity than their counterparts with citizen mothers and that demographic characteristics such as being Latina, levels of maternal education, and large household size explain about half of the difference in rates. © 2008 Wiley Periodicals, Inc.

Funding for this research was provided to A. Kalil by a Faculty Scholars Award from the William T. Grant Foundation, a Changing Faces of America's Children Young Scholars Award from the Foundation for Child Development, and a Research Development Grant from the U.S. Department of Agriculture, Economic Research Service. We thank Heather Royer for helpful comments.

Children of immigrants are the fastest-growing component of the child population. Although immigrants comprise only 11% of the total population, children of immigrants represent 22% of children under 6 years of age in the United States (Capps, Fix, Ost, Reardon-Anderson, & Passel, 2004). The 1996 federal welfare reform law introduced, among other things, broad restrictions on immigrants' eligibility for many health and social service programs, including cash welfare assistance (TANF), Food Stamps, and subsidized health insurance. Caseloads for these benefit programs have fallen dramatically in the wake of welfare reform (Blank, 2002), but the declines have been steeper for immigrants than for native-born citizens (Fix & Passel, 1999), even when immigrant families remain eligible for assistance.

In light of their more limited use of government assistance programs, it is not surprising that immigrant families are poorer and suffer more material hardships than their native counterparts (Capps, 2001). In particular, after welfare reform, children of immigrant noncitizens experienced more persistent and higher levels of food insecurity compared to the children of citizens (Van Hook & Balistreri, 2006).

Food insecurity, defined as limited or uncertain access to enough nutritious and safe food or limited or uncertain ability to acquire acceptable foods in socially acceptable ways (Bickel, Nord, Price, Hamilton, & Cook 2000, is prevalent among many low-income families. In 2002, about 11% of American households were classified as food insecure (Wilde & Nord, 2005), but the rate was higher in households with children (18%), poor families (37%), and in Black (24%) and Hispanic (22%) households (Nord, Andrews, & Carlson, 2003). Notably, a recent study of low-income legal immigrants in California, Texas, and Illinois reported rates of food insecurity of 80% (Kasper, Gupta, Tran, Cook, & Meyers, 2000). As measured by the U.S. Food Security Scale (Bickel, Nord, Price, Hamilton, & Cook, 2000), food security is considered a marker for the adequacy and stability of the household food supply over the past 12 months for active, healthy living for all household members (Bickel et al., 2000). Clearly, however, there is wide variation in low-income families' experience of food insecurity, given that not all children in low-income families are food insecure.

A number of studies has shown the potential negative impact of food insecurity on children's health and development. Food insecurity is associated with poor child outcomes in the realms of physical health as well as psychological and academic functioning (Alaimo, Olson, & Frongillo, 2001; Casey et al., 2006; Dunifon & Kowaleski-Jones, 2003; Slack & Yoo, 2005; Winicki & Jemison, 2003). Adverse impacts of food insecurity on young children's health and development are important given the linkages between early childhood circumstances and later life outcomes (Case, Fertig, & Paxson, 2003). Food insecurity may be a particular concern for the young low-income children of immigrants, given their already elevated risk for poor health (Huang, Yu, & Ledsky, 2006).

NEW DIRECTIONS FOR CHILD AND ADOLESCENT DEVELOPMENT • DOI: 10.1002/cd

Few studies have aimed to explain food insecurity among low-income families, and even fewer have focused specifically on low-income immigrant families and how or why they differ from their native counterparts. It is not surprising that standard demographic characteristics such as differing levels of program participation, education, employment, and income are important determinants of food insecurity within low-income populations. Given important differences in such socioeconomic characteristics between low-income native and immigrant populations, it is plausible to hypothesize that these variables would account for the higher levels of food insecurity among immigrant populations. However, in immigrant populations additional factors may account for their higher levels of food insecurity, including parents' citizenship status and parents' integration into the community. Immigrant noncitizens are less likely to be aware of community programs and health services compared to their native and naturalized citizen counterparts (Huang et al., 2006; Yu, Huang, Schwalberg, & Kogan, 2005). Immigrant parents are also more likely than their native counterparts to be limited English proficient (LEP). This lack of social and linguistic integration could result in higher rates of food insecurity if families are unable to make use of community resources that could ease material hardships.

We used a national data set that contains an unusually wide range of potentially important variables to explain the differential rates of food insecurity between low-income native and immigrant populations, allowing us to gain a deeper perspective on the factors that predict food insecurity among low-income families and, in particular, the key factors that explain differences in rates of food insecurity among the children of immigrant noncitizens, children of immigrant citizens, and children of natives.

Background

Rates of food insecurity are higher in the low-income immigrant population compared to the low-income native population (Capps, 2001; Van Hook & Balistreri, 2006). It is well documented that low-income immigrant families have less education, work at lower-quality jobs (as defined by wage rates and benefits), and are less likely to participate in government benefit programs than their native counterparts. For example, in 2002, the individual Food Stamps Program participation rate for citizen children living with noncitizen adults was 44%, compared to 70% for all eligible children (Cunnynham, 2004). Higher levels of education allow individuals to secure better-remunerated jobs with better benefits, thus providing more income and insurance to the household. Employment that provides greater earnings and insurance can boost the resources available for consumption, which can, in turn, alleviate food insecurity. Alaimo, Briefel, Frongillo, and Olson (1998) found that income is negatively related to food insufficiency among low-income individuals in the NHANES III. Gundersen and Gruber (2001 reported similar findings. Finally, the Food Stamp Program has been shown to alleviate food insecurity (Gundersen & Oliveira, 2001).

Beyond demographic characteristics that may increase the risk of food insecurity among low-income immigrant populations, psychological and family factors may also play a role. The transition to a new society is a major life change that could place a high degree of stress on foreign-born noncitizen mothers of young children. Such stress could potentially increase maternal depression. Depression and stress may, in turn, interfere with a parent's ability to work or to manage a household or a monthly food budget on a limited income. Casey and colleagues (2004) show that maternal depression is associated with higher rates of food insecurity in low-income populations. Some research suggests that whereas Mexican-born immigrants are less likely to exhibit frank psychopathology than their U.S.-born ethnic counterparts, they are more likely to have unexplained somatic symptoms, which are generally taken as symptoms of distress (Escobar, Waitzkin, Silver, Gara, & Holman, 1998).

Parenting skills and knowledge may also be important correlates of food insecurity insofar as they reflect an ability to effectively manage a household, including its budget. Several studies have found that more acculturated Latinos make greater use of preventive health services (Lara, Gamboa, Kahramanian, Morales, & Bautista, 2005). With respect to children's preventive health care, this type of behavior could proxy for parents' knowledge and skills (especially if insurance coverage is held constant). In addition, Dumka, Roosa, and Jackson (1997) suggested that less-acculturated Mexican immigrant mothers demonstrated poorer parenting skills vis-à-vis their more acculturated and Mexican American counterparts. We do not know of any studies that have assessed the association of mothers' mental health or parenting behaviors with household-level food insecurity. It is important to bear in mind, however, that the associations between food insecurity and mothers' mental health or parenting behaviors may run in both directions.

Despite knowing these basic differences between low-income native and immigrant families, it remains unknown if a standard set of demographic and socioeconomic characteristics, or even an augmented set of factors that also includes parental well-being and parenting characteristics, will account for the differential rates of food insecurity in low-income native and immigrant populations. We propose that an important characteristic of the low-income immigrant population—one that has not been well-studied in relation to food insecurity—is its relative lack of social integration. This stems in many respects from the language barriers faced by many non-English speakers. A lack of English ability could impede the development of communication skills that enable immigrant parents to better negotiate with the bureaucracies of government assistance programs or private charities (Huang et al., 2006). Low-income immigrant mothers, for example, are less likely to be involved in their children's schools and other civic organizations compared to low-income native mothers (Crosnoe, 2006). Social isolation, which may result from linguistic isolation, may make it difficult to learn about, develop, and successfully execute coping strategies to deal with material hardship and ward off food insecurity. In one recent local study of Latino families in Chicago, more than half of the food-insufficient mothers (most of whom were Mexican immigrants) did not know where to seek food if they were short of money (Chavez, Telleen, & Kim, 2007). Parents who interact with and trust their neighbors may be able to shop more effectively for food (e.g., by borrowing a car or getting a ride to the store) or to approach or rely on neighbors for assistance (e.g., by borrowing or exchanging services for food). Social capital (a measure of trust, reciprocity, and social networks) has been associated with household food security in low-income households, independent of socioeconomic factors (Martin, Rogers, Cook, & Joseph, 2004). However, the role of co-ethnic enclaves has been implicated in the relatively poorer economic outcomes of immigrants with limited human capital (Borjas, 2006). Thus, to the extent that high levels of social capital correlate positively with more compact co-ethnic immigrant social networks that interact little with the economic mainstream, such a measure might actually be positively correlated with food insecurity.

In light of the potential importance of social integration, we propose two key distinctions. First, it is important to distinguish among children who are born in the United States to foreign-born parents from those children who are themselves born abroad. Second, it is important to distinguish among children of immigrant parents of differing citizenship statuses. By definition in our data, children who are born abroad are more recent arrivals to the United States. Newly arrived parents, who likely maintain strong ties to their country of origin, will have had less time to accumulate the social capital and know-how that could help them secure material support in times of need. Similarly, immigrant mothers who have not completed the path to citizenship are presumably less socially integrated than their immigrant counterparts who have been naturalized.

The relevance of citizenship, recency of arrival, and social capital are particularly important in the post-welfare reform era. Immigrants were the target of many of the most stringent federal reforms under the Personal Responsibility and Work Opportunity Reconciliation Act (PRWORA; Pub. L. 104-193, 1996). Prior to the reforms enacted in 1996, legal immigrants and their children were generally eligible for public benefits under the same terms as citizens (although undocumented immigrants have never been eligible for benefits). However, by the late 1990s, immigrant families faced a vastly different policy environment—one marked by a potentially confusing set of rules concerning their eligibility to receive public assistance. The so-called chilling effect hypothesis maintains that immigrant families are reluctant to access public assistance because of confusion about eligibility and fear of the potential consequences for family members (Shields & Behrman, 2004). Parents who are not citizens may not be aware of their

NEW DIRECTIONS FOR CHILD AND ADOLESCENT DEVELOPMENT • DOI: 10.1002/cd

U.S.-born children's eligibility for important benefits. Immigrant parents may also believe that seeking assistance for their eligible children will hinder other family members' efforts to obtain citizenship or legal status or their ability to re-enter and stay in the United States (Capps, 2001; Fix & Passel, 1999). Immigrant parents' high likelihood of being LEP could also contribute to their misunderstanding or confusion regarding the policy changes or their eligibility for programs. Thus, having access to neighbors one can rely on and trust, or being integrated into social networks that could impart useful information, might be especially important to low-income immigrants in times of heightened policy flux.

In summary, a variety of studies has linked demographic, human capital, and personal characteristics to rates of food insecurity in low-income populations. Food insecurity is an important correlate of poor health and developmental outcomes in children. Low-income immigrant families, compared to their native counterparts, are at greater risk of food insecurity and, in general, have worse profiles on the range of socioeconomic and demographic factors that correlate with food insecurity. One might reasonably assume that these differences in socioeconomic characteristics explain the observed differences in rates of food insecurity in the different populations. Surprisingly, little research has answered this question. We speculate that socioeconomic and personal characteristics are not sufficient to explain the gaps in food insecurity and that attention to immigrants' social integration may be an important component of differences. We address this point by distinguishing among foreign-born children with citizen versus noncitizen mothers as well as native-born children with foreign-born citizen versus noncitizen mothers, and by drawing on measures that plausibly indicate social integration to explain any remaining differences in food insecurity in the different populations, after socioeconomic and personal characteristics have been accounted for.

Sample

This study used data from the second wave of the public use version of the Early Childhood Longitudinal Study-Kindergarten Cohort (ECLS-K), a nationally representative sample of approximately 22,000 children enrolled in about 1,000 kindergartens during the 1998–1999 school years. The children were on average 75 months old at the second wave. Our dependent variable (food insecurity) was unavailable in the first wave. We restricted our sample to those families below 200% poverty threshold in Wave 2 (based on household income and size); this was designed to target households at risk for food insecurity as well as to compare immigrant children (many of whom are low income) to their low-income native counterparts. A sample of 6,445 was obtained. Further deletion of the data was due to missing values on the dependent variable and grouping variables (defined in the following section). Our final sample size was 6,068.

NEW DIRECTIONS FOR CHILD AND ADOLESCENT DEVELOPMENT • DOI: 10.1002/cd

Variables

Dependent Variable. Parents in the ECLS-K completed the 18-item U.S. Household Standard Food-Security/Hunger Survey Module created by the U.S. Department of Agriculture (USDA; Bickel, Nord, Price, Hamilton, & Cook, 2000). Food insecurity was captured at the household level and assessed experiences in the past 12 months such as running out of food, perceptions that the food was of inadequate quality or quantity, and reduced food intake—all due to financial constraints. In our analysis, the dependent variable was a dummy variable indicating whether the family was food insecure or not. This measure was constructed from the four-part food security status variable (precoded in ECLS-K and described in Nord & Bickel, 2002), which reported the family as being *food secure, food insecure without hunger, food insecure with moderate hunger,* or *food insecure with severe hunger.* We grouped the last three responses together as food insecure (1/0), which means that the parent answered affirmatively to fewer than three items on the 18-point scale. It is important to note, however, that families in the omitted group (*not food insecure*) may still have experienced worries that food would run out or have experienced actual food shortages.

Defining Groups. One of the strengths of this study is that our data allowed us to go beyond the oft-used distinction of "children of immigrants" (Hernandez, 2004) and to categorize different types of immigrant families depending on the parental birthplaces and mother's citizenship status. Information on the mother's birthplace was available from the second, fourth, and fifth waves of the survey. Data on the father's birthplace was available in the fourth and fifth waves. We first transformed these variables into binary variables. Parents who were born in the United States were coded as U.S.-born and others were coded as foreign-born. We considered those who were born in U.S. unincorporated territories (that is, American Samoa, Guam, Puerto Rico, Northern Mariana Islands, U.S. Virgin Islands) as U.S.-born. To minimize the possibility of misreporting, we used all three waves of information (two waves for father). In case of inconsistencies across waves, the solutions were as follows: If a mother reported being U.S.-born in any two waves and foreign-born in the remaining wave, we assigned her as U.S.-born. If a mother reported being foreign-born in any two waves and U.S.-born in the remaining wave, we assigned her as foreign-born. If only two waves of data were available (by definition, this includes all fathers) and there was an inconsistency in his or her country of birth (U.S.- or foreign-born), we assigned them as foreign-born.

The second variable in our group definition was mothers' citizenship. We only considered mother's citizenship because mothers are usually the primary caregivers in the household and there were substantial numbers of single-mother families in our low-income sample. Dichotomous variables of mother's citizenship were available at Waves 4, 5, and 6. However, unlike birthplace, one's citizenship does change. Using citizenship information

NEW DIRECTIONS FOR CHILD AND ADOLESCENT DEVELOPMENT • DOI: 10.1002/cd

from the fourth wave to determine mother's citizenship status in the second wave (i.e., when our outcomes measure of food insecurity is assessed) may have run the risk of underestimating the number of noncitizen mothers. That is, mothers who were not U.S. citizens in the second wave may have become U.S. citizens in the fourth wave. We identified 127 mothers who were not U.S. citizens in Wave 4, but who became U.S. citizens by Wave 6. Therefore, we suspect the number of mothers who became citizens between the second and fourth wave was very small. However, even if we had underestimated the size of the noncitizen population, our coefficients in the regressions would have been an underestimate of the risks facing noncitizens. Our estimates were relatively conservative in this sense.

Using information on mothers' citizenship and parental birth places, we created the following seven mutually exclusive groups: (1) child and parents foreign-born, noncitizen mother ($n = 144$); (2) child and parents foreign-born, citizen mother ($n = 23$); (3) child U.S.-born, parents foreign-born, noncitizen mother ($n = 694$); (4) child U.S.-born, parents foreign-born, citizen mother ($n = 398$); (5) child U.S.-born, only one parent foreign-born, noncitizen mother ($n = 40$); (6) child U.S.-born, only one parent foreign-born, citizen mother ($n = 232$); and (7) child, parents U.S.-born ($n = 4,537$).

Because we did not use current marital status as a criterion in creating our groups, all seven groups contained both single-parent and two-parent families. That is, having information on both mothers and fathers did not preclude the child from living in a single-parent family.

Demographics. Our analysis contained a series of demographic variables. Child's race was represented by a series of dummy variables that distinguished White, Latino, African American, and children of other races. We grouped Asian American, Native American, Pacific Islanders, mixed races, and cases where race is uncertain in the other races category due to the relatively small size of each of these groups (around 3%) in our sample. Given the heterogeneity of this group, however, caution should be exercised in interpreting its coefficient in the regression analysis. Mothers' employment status was coded in four categories—full-time, part-time, unemployed, and out of labor force (this is the omitted group). Mothers' education was also coded in multiple categories (with "no high school degree" serving as the omitted group). We also included a dummy variable for whether the child lived in a single-parent family (these were almost all single-mother families) and a continuous measure of family size.

Income and Program Participation. Family income plays a central role in determining the economic resources of a family. We included a continuous income variable measured by thousands of dollars in our regression. In addition to income, welfare programs affect economic well-being among low-income families. We therefore included the Aid to Families with Dependent Children (AFDC) program and Food Stamp Program participation during the past 12 months as covariates. In addition, we added two controls to represent resources the family may have had available that would have freed up other resources to direct toward food. The first variable indicated the child's participation in the free lunch program at school and the second indicated whether the child had health insurance. All program participation variables were coded one if the respondent took part in the program and zero otherwise.

Parent mental health and behavior. We included three variables we considered as proxies of parental well-being and behavior. First, we included a dummy variable for maternal depression. This survey question was originally worded as, "How often during the past week have you felt depressed?" with possible responses including *never, some of the time, a moderate amount of time*, and *most of the time*. We recoded this measure into a dummy variable where *never* = 0 and all other responses = 1. Second, we used a binary indicator of a routine health check for the child in the past 12 months as another proxy for parenting behaviors. A value of one indicated that the child had been brought to a routine health visit within the past 12 months and zero if not. Finally, we constructed a mealtime routine score from a set of measures recording how many days a family had dinner and breakfast together and how many days they had dinner and breakfast at a regular time during the week. We relied on this measure as an indicator of how organized and attentive mothers were in managing household routines (and possibly, by extension, their family's food budget and plan). The actual mealtime routine score ranged from 1 to 7.

Social Integration. In the final set of predictor variables, we sought to control for the extent to which household food insecurity was associated with the family's social integration. First, we aimed to capture such an effect using two measures of the family's connections to the community: a subjective measure of mothers' perception of the level of support in the community served by their child's school and a subjective measure of her perceptions of the safety of the neighborhood. The respondents were originally asked one question about whether they thought the community served by their child's school was supportive, with response scales ranging from 1 = *strongly disagree* to 5 = *strongly agree*. We transformed this variable to a binary variable by coding *strongly agree* and *agree* as one and all other responses as zero. The neighborhood safety question was originally coded on a 3-point response scale asking mothers how safe they thought it was for children to play outside during the day in the neighborhood, where 1 = *not at all safe*, 2 = *somewhat safe*, and 3 = *very safe*. We coded this variable as one if the respondent answered *very safe;* otherwise this was coded as zero.

As a measure of potential linguistic isolation, we also included a variable asking the mother how often she spoke to her child in English. Responses ranged from 1 = *speak English only* to 4 = *very often speak language other than English*. This measure is potentially reflective of the extent to which immigrant families are linguistically integrated into society and civic organizations. Finally, we included a constructed measure of the mothers' proportion of time in the United States over their life course. To create this variable, we first measured each immigrant mother's length of stay in the

United States by subtracting her age of entry into the United States from her current age. Next, we computed the ratio of her length of stay to her current age. Intuitively, this new variable represented the proportion of time of an immigrant mother's stay in the United States over her life course. By default, a native mother would spend all her time in the United States. We therefore assigned the value of one to all native-born mothers on this variable.

Statistical Procedures

We used Probit regression to account for the binary nature of our dependent variable. Our analyses proceeded as follows. We began by regressing food insecurity on the demographic variables in Model 1. In the second model (Model 2), we added income and program participation variables. Model 3 included the measures proxying for mothers' well-being and parental behavior. In Model 4, we added the four measures of social integration. To correct for the clustered nature of the data, we used a robust standard error estimator. We also applied the Wave 2 survey sampling weight to all analyses.

All missing values were dealt with by one of two methods. For categorical variables, we coded the missing cases into a missing category and included a missing data dummy in the regression (Eberwein, Ham, & LaLonde, 1997). For continuous variables, we imputed missing values. We first regressed the to-be-imputed variable on all other independent variables (demographics, parenting, social integration, and so on) for cases where data were not missing and obtained the coefficient estimates. Next, we used these estimates to generate predicted values of the to-be-imputed variable. Lastly, we assigned the predicted values to the missing variable. By doing so, we retained our sample size of 6,068 in all regression analyses. Most of the variables in our analysis contained only a small number of missing values, ranging from 0% to 5%. Two variables, however, had a larger proportion of missing values: mother's employment status (14%) and the measure of support in the community served by the child's school (21%).

Descriptive Statistics

Table 4.1 presents descriptive statistics across all groups of children. The rate of household food insecurity among low-income native-born children with native-born parents is 8%. Two groups—foreign-born children with foreign-born parents and a noncitizen mother, as well as U.S.-born children with all foreign-born parents and a noncitizen mother—had significantly higher rates of food insecurity (20%) compared to low-income native-born children with native-born parents (hereafter called *native families*). Differences between other types of immigrant families and native families were not significant (we did not put too much stock in the results for the group of foreign-born children with citizen mothers or the group with one foreign-born parent and a noncitizen mother due to small sample sizes). Of interest, however, is that a large group of children with both foreign-born parents/citizen mothers had a comparable rate of food insecurity compared to native families.

In general, the descriptive characteristics show that children with noncitizen mothers (compared to children in native families and those with foreign-born citizen mothers) face a number of risk factors that might explain their higher likelihood of being food insecure. For example, they are more likely to have mothers with very limited education and employment and to have lower rates of health insurance coverage, TANF use, and Food Stamps program participation. Such children are also significantly more likely to have a mother who is depressed. In addition, foreign-born children with noncitizen mothers are less likely to have had a routine doctor visit in the past 12 months. Children with noncitizen mothers are also the least likely to have mothers who speak to them exclusively in English (they are also much more likely to be Latino than native-born children) and their mothers have stayed a smaller share of their lifetimes in the United States compared with mothers who are citizens. Finally, children of noncitizen mothers are the most likely to rate their neighborhoods as not safe.

Multivariate Analysis

Table 4.2 presents the marginal effects from the probit regressions of food insecurity on the independent variables. Model 1 controlled only for demographic variables. Recall that in the univariate comparisons, the difference in rates of food insecurity for children with noncitizen mothers compared to children of native mothers was about 12 percentage points (i.e., 20% in the former groups compared to 8% in the latter). Here, we see that with the addition of the set of demographic characteristics, this differential is reduced to about six percentage points (for the larger group of native-born children with noncitizen mothers on whom we focus in these multivariate regressions). Interestingly, however, the group of children with one foreign-born parent and a U.S. citizen mother was significantly less likely to be food insecure compared to natives once the demographic characteristics are controlled.

Among this important set of variables, several show significant associations with food insecurity in the expected direction, including mothers' education and household size. Households in which mothers had the least amount of education were the most likely to be food insecure, as were those with more household members. Latino families were also significantly more likely to be food insecure than Whites. Thus, several of the distinguishing characteristics of immigrant families with noncitizen mothers (low education, Latino, and larger household size) correlated with food insecurity and explained a substantial share of the gap in the prevalence of food insecurity in this population compared to households with native-born mothers.

NEW DIRECTIONS FOR CHILD AND ADOLESCENT DEVELOPMENT • DOI: 10.1002/cd

Table 4.1. Descriptive Statistics (Weighted)

	Child FB, Mom Noncitizen (N = 144)	Child FB, Mom U.S. Citizen (N = 23)	Both Parents, FB Mom Noncitizen (N = 694)	Both Parents, FB Mom U.S. Citizen (N = 398)	One Parent, FB Mom Noncitizen (N = 40)	One Parent FB, Mom U.S. Citizen (N = 232)	Both Parents U.S. Born (N = 4537)
Food insecure (%)	20	20	20	10	7	6	8
White (%)	5	28	4	12	6	30	50
Latino (%)	85	26	86	57	89	57	12
African American (%)	6	29	5	7	2	5	30
Other races (%)	5	16	5	24	3	8	8
Mom's employment:							
Fulltime (%)	26	51	27	41	32	40	43
Part-time (%)	14	6	14	16	24	21	20
Unemployed (%)	3	0	4	6	0	3	8
Out of labor force (%)	56	42	54	37	44	37	30
Mom's education:							
HS Dropout or less (%)	46	23	62	31	38	27	21
HS, GED (%)	27	23	26	35	37	37	43
Some college (%)	17	35	8	25	23	29	31
College or above (%)	10	19	3	10	2	7	5
Average household size	5.26	4.66	5.33	5.10	4.69	5.14	4.74

New Directions for Child and Adolescent Development • DOI: 10.1002/cd

Single parent family (%)	20	41	32	34	43	30	54
Income	$17,062	$20,371	$18,029	$22,323	$19,757	$22,078	$19,650
Insurance coverage (%)	46	73	71	82	75	83	88
AFDC Recipient (%)	7	17	11	12	2	11	14
Free school lunch (%)	66	47	76	61	75	62	60
Food Stamp recipient (%)	13	16	26	22	23	26	38
Mom depressed (%)	48	24	42	34	46	27	36
Routine doctor visit (%)	83	90	89	92	100	94	95
Mealtime routine score	5.52	6.00	5.22	5.22	5.14	5.33	5.42
Mother's language to child:							
Speaks English only (%)	8	36	11	18	12	45	90
Sometimes speaks language other than English (%)	4	4	4	18	13	21	6
Often speaks language other than English (%)	12	22	13	18	15	16	2
Very often speaks language other than English (%)	76	40	71	46	61	17	2
Neighborhood safety (%)	41	62	44	56	33	56	63
Supportive community (%)	80	93	78	80	82	80	81
Proportion stayed in the U.S. over the life course (%)	15	37	34	50	40	91	100

Note: FB = Foreign-born; HS = high school; GED = general education diploma; AFDC = Aid to Families with Dependent Children Program.

Table 4.2. Marginal Effects From Probit Regression Results for Food Insecurity

	Model 1	Model 2	Model 3	Model 4
	(Standard Errors in parentheses; N = 6,068)			
Child FB, noncitizen mother	.075* (.041)	.062 (.039)	.035 (.035)	.046 (.061)
Child FB, mother U.S. citizen	.081 (.098)	.081 (.096)	.106 (.099)	.123 (.111)
Both parents FB, noncitizen mother	.063** (.022)	.065** (.023)	.053** (.022)	.065 (.045)
Both parents FB, mother U.S. citizen	−.035 (.021)	−.025 (.022)	−.029 (.021)	−.020 (.032)
One parent FB, noncitizen mother	−.087* (.041)	−.077 (.044)	−.078 (.041)	−.080 (.042)
One parent FB, mother U.S. citizen	−.077** (.021)	−.073** (.021)	−.067** (.020)	−.066** (.021)
Latino	.038* (.018)	.024 (.018)	.019 (.017)	.013 (.019)
African American	−.009 (.014)	−.031 (.014)	−.041** (.014)	−.051*** (.013)
Others	.016 (.019)	−.008 (.018)	−.004 (.018)	−.006 (.018)
Fulltime	.011 (.013)	.037** (.014)	.031* (.014)	.030* (.013)
Part-time	-.007 (.017)	.004 (.017)	.001 (.016)	−.002 (.016)
Unemployed	.013 (.024)	.002 (.023)	−.001 (.022)	−.004 (.022)
HS Diploma or equivalent	−.026* (.013)	−.014 (.013)	−.010 (.013)	−.006 (.013)
Some college or vocational training	−.038** (.014)	−.015 (.015)	−.001 (.015)	.002 (.015)
College or above	−.109*** (.016)	−.080** (.020)	−.066* (.022)	−.062* (.022)
Household size	.010** (.003)	.013*** (.003)	.014*** (.003)	−.014*** (.003)
Single-parent family	.059*** (.011)	.017 (.012)	.006 (.012)	.005 (.012)
Income (per thousand dollars)		−.003*** (.000)	−.003*** (.000)	−.003*** (.000)
Insurance coverage		−.036* (.016)	−.026 (.015)	−.026 (.015)
AFDC recipient		.045** (.017)	.049** (.018)	.043** (.017)

(continued on next page)

Table 4.2. Marginal Effects From Probit Regression Results for Food Insecurity

| | (Standard Errors in parentheses; N = 6,068) | | | |
	Model 1	Model 2	Model 3	Model 4
Children receive free school lunch		−.001 (.012)	−.005 (.012)	−.004 (.011)
Food Stamp recipient		.049*** (.015)	.045*** (.014)	.041** (.014)
Mother depressed			.138*** (.012)	.132*** (.012)
Routine doctor visit			−.078*** (.023)	−.078*** (.023)
Mealtime routine			−.017*** (.004)	−.015*** (.004)
Speak English only				.010 (.022)
Sometimes speak language other than English				.015 (.028)
Often speak language other than English				−.022 (.025)
Neighborhood safety				−.067*** (.011)
Supportive community				.004 (.014)
Proportion of stay in the U.S. over the life course				.015 (.048)

Note: Both parents U.S. born, White, out of labor force, HS dropout, very often speak language other than English categories were omitted. FB = Foreign-born; HS = high school; AFDC = Aid to Families with Dependent Children

*p < .05. **p < .01. ***p < .001.

In Model 2, we controlled for economic resources and program participation. Doing so did not change the coefficients and the significance level of food insecurity across groups very much. These results suggest that economic resources and program participation explain little of the remaining gap in the rate of food insecurity across groups. At the same time, income did appear to matter. Our estimates show that an increase of income of $10,000 would reduce the probability of food insecurity by three percentage points. Participation in welfare programs—AFDC and Food Stamps—showed positive marginal effects on food insecurity, illustrating the adverse selection into these programs (Gundersen & Oliveira, 2001). In contrast, households in which children had health insurance were less likely to be food insecure.

In Model 3, we added three proxies of parental well being and behavior —maternal depression, routine doctor visit, and mealtime routines. Doing so also did not change the coefficients and the significance level of food insecurity across groups very much, with the exception that adding these measures reduced the coefficient on child foreign-born/noncitizen mother by about 40%, to 3.5 percentage points. At the same time, these measures highly correlated with food insecurity. For example, having a depressed mother was associated with an increased likelihood of being food insecure by about 14 percentage points (the strongest correlate among all of our measures). In contrast, families in which parents had brought their children for a routine health check within the past 12 months were eight percentage points less likely to be food insecure. Regular mealtime routines had a moderate negative association with food insecurity.

Finally, Model 4 added four proxies of a family's degree of social integration. These measures did not explain any of the residual gap in rates of food insecurity across populations and among these variables; only outdoor safety was significantly correlated with food insecurity. Living in a community perceived as safe was associated with a decrease in a family's probability of food insecurity by approximately seven percentage points.

Summary and Conclusions

There are several significant aspects of this study. First, we used data from a nationally representative survey to assess patterns of food insecurity in immigrant children and their families. Second, we were able to draw on information about children and parents' nativity and mothers' citizenship status to create a more comprehensive grouping system than previous studies have done. Third, our data provide an unusually rich set of putative mediators to more fully explore the reasons why young low-income children in immigrant families experience higher levels of food insecurity than their native counterparts. At the same time, our analyses were based on cross-sectional data. As such, even though we illustrated several interesting and substantively important associations between the predictor variables and food insecurity, reverse causality is always a possibility.

Our analysis shows that children with foreign-born mothers, but only those with a noncitizen mother, have higher levels of food insecurity than their native counterparts. The magnitude of the difference between the two populations is sizeable: children with noncitizen mothers are more than twice as likely to be food insecure as their counterparts with native-born parents. In contrast, low-income families in which foreign-born mothers are citizens are at approximately the same risk for food insecurity compared to their counterparts with native-born mothers.

Our first main finding is that demographic characteristics (race, maternal employment and education, and household structure) account for about half of the difference in rates of food insecurity between children with native and noncitizen mothers. Among this set of measures, low maternal education, being Latina, and having a larger household size were all significantly correlated with food insecurity. These variables, in turn, were far more likely to characterize immigrant households with noncitizen mothers compared to households with native mothers.

These findings raise interesting questions for future research. Larger households clearly suggest more mouths to feed. Holding income constant (as we did here) means that the same amount of food will go less far in meeting each householder's needs. In contrast, low education might translate into a lack of knowledge about food banks or other ways to alleviate material hardship or strategies to make ends meet. It would be interesting for future research to investigate why Latina mothers are more likely to be food insecure than their White counterparts. This may suggest a role of cultural mismatch between service-providing organizations and the families that need those services. In this instance, in-depth qualitative research could go a long way toward understanding what are undoubtedly nuanced phenomena associated with interpersonal interactions.

At the same time, the size of the association of the Latina variable decreased across models (refer to Table 4.2) suggesting that it is correlated with other measures in our model that also predict food insecurity. For example, the association was only half as strong in Model 2, which added the income and program participation variables. Lacking health insurance was more characteristic of immigrant families with noncitizen mothers (most of whom are Latina) compared to families with native mothers, and lack of health insurance was, in turn, associated with higher levels of food insecurity. Thus, part of the Latina effect is really a lack of health insurance effect, which presumably indicates something about the families' expenditures and consumption because income was held constant.

Our second main finding is that, having explained about half of the differential rate of food insecurity between families with noncitizen mothers and those with native mothers, neither family economic resources nor program participation variables, nor parental characteristics explain much of the residual gap across these populations. Thus, mothers' citizenship status plays an important role in low-income children's food insecurity, but in ways that we are not able to fully understand with the survey data we have available here.

These questions thus remain important ones for future work. It is possible that noncitizen parents are at a higher risk of alienation from systems of support that are available to low-income and vulnerable populations in the United States, although whatever factors these might be, they are not clearly linked to the level of support in the community served by their child's school, their perceptions of safety in their neighborhood, and some factors related to acculturation, such as English language use with their children or length of time in the United States.

What else might characterize the experience of low-income immigrant families with and without a citizen mother that are associated with food insecurity? One factor might be differences in the quality of social networks and the resources that such networks provide. These networks could differ among those who have yet to become citizens (and could in fact, make the difference between becoming and not becoming a citizen), or one's networks could change after becoming a citizen. Future work could rely on quantitative and qualitative approaches to understanding this question.

Relatedly, future work could examine the process and meaning of becoming a citizen. For example, the process of applying for citizenship may involve repeated contact with governmental officials or other people. This, in turn, may give families new and important information, or may help familiarize families with the process of interacting with government officials and service providers, all of which could provide material, social, and cultural advantages that could help mitigate exposure to food insecurity.

Future work should explore these questions using longitudinal data with analytic techniques designed to rule out selection bias. For example, for the process of becoming a citizen to play a causal role in food insecurity, one should observe changes in food security over time within families whose mothers become citizens. One could rely on the multiple waves of the ECLS-K to answer this question. If such changes are not observed, these associations may simply be driven by unmeasured factors that differentiate these two populations, which also drive the differences in rates of food insecurity.

Finally, given these alarmingly high rates of food insecurity in low-income immigrant populations, one clear direction for future work is to understand whether and in what ways this marker of material hardship is associated with children's development, and especially whether these patterns are similar or different for children with citizen versus noncitizen mothers. In our data, the majority of the noncitizen immigrant families were from Latin America. Our sample was not large enough to separate this group from Asian or other immigrant populations and to see if the same associations hold in different groups of low-income immigrants with noncitizen mothers. This is another important goal for future work, perhaps relying on high-quality local data that oversample Asian and other non-Latin American immigrant populations.

The immigrant children who were the focus of this study are America's future workers and parents. The productivity of the nation will increasingly rest on their achievement, health, and integration in their communities. It is thus imperative to understand the early life circumstances that shape whether and how these children reach their fullest potential, especially in an increasingly diverse population. If barriers are identified, there may be a role for public policy to intervene. Clearly, more work is needed to understand why immigrant families with noncitizen mothers experience such high rates of food insecurity. To the extent that differences in families' experiences of material hardship and food insecurity are associated, ultimately, with differences in children's health and well being, it will be critical to develop culturally sensitive outreach programs and the development of other mechanisms to help all families receive assistance to meet their needs and ensure their children's economic security and healthy development.

References

Alaimo, K., Briefel, R., Frongillo, E., & Olson, C. (1998). Food insufficiency exists in the United States: Results from the Third National Health and Nutrition Examination Survey (NHANES III). *American Journal of Public Health, 88,* 419–426.

Alaimo, K., Olson, C., & Frongillo, E. (2001). Food insufficiency and American school-aged children's cognitive, academic, and psychosocial development. *Pediatrics, 108,* 44–53.

Bickel, G., Nord, M., Price, C., Hamilton, W., & Cook, J. (2000). *Guide to measuring household food security, Revised 2000.* Alexandria, VA: U.S. Department of Agriculture, Food and Nutrition Service.

Blank, R. (2002). Evaluating welfare reform in the United States. *Journal of Economic Literature, 40,* 1105–1166.

Borjas, G. (2006). Native internal migration and the labor market impact of immigration. *Journal of Human Resources, XLI,* 221–258.

Capps, R. (2001, February). *Hardship among children of immigrants: Findings from the 1999 National Survey of America's Families, Series B* (No. B–29). Washington, DC: The Urban Institute.

Capps, R., Fix, M., Ost, J., Reardon-Anderson, J., & Passel, J. (2004). *The health and well-being of young children of immigrants.* Washington, DC: The Urban Institute.

Case, A., Fertig, A., & Paxson, C. (2003). *From cradle to grave? The lasting impact of childhood health and circumstance* (NBER Working Paper #9788). Cambridge, MA: National Bureau of Economic Research.

Casey, P., Goolsby, S., Berkowitz, C., Frank, D., Cook, J., Cutts, D., et al. (2004). Maternal depression, changing public assistance, food security, and child health status. *Pediatrics, 113,* 298–304.

Casey, P., Simpson, P., Gossett, J., Bogle, M., Champagne, C., Connell, C., et al. (2006). The association of child and household food insecurity with childhood overweight status. *Pediatrics, 118,* 1406–1413.

Chavez, N., Telleen, S., & Kim, Y. (2007). Food insufficiency in urban Latino families. *Journal of Immigrant and Minority Health, 9,* 197–204.

Crosnoe, R. (2006). *Mexican Roots, American Schools: Helping Mexican immigrant children succeed.* Stanford, CA: Stanford University Press.

Cunnynham, K. (2004, September). *Trends in Food Stamp Program participation rates: 1999 to 2002.* Alexandria, VA: U.S. Department of Agriculture, Food and Nutrition Service.

Dumka, L., Roosa, M., & Jackson, K. (1997). Risk, conflict, mothers' parenting, and children's adjustment in low-income, Mexican immigrant, and Mexican American families. *Journal of Marriage and the Family, 59,* 309–323.

Dunifon, R., & Kowaleski-Jones, L. (2003). Associations between participation in the National School Lunch Program, food insecurity, and child well-being. *Social Service Review, 77,* 72–92.

Eberwein, C., Ham, J., & LaLonde, R. (1997). The impact of being offered and receiving classroom training on the employment histories of disadvantaged women: Evidence from experimental data. *Review of Economic Studies, 64,* 655–682.

NEW DIRECTIONS FOR CHILD AND ADOLESCENT DEVELOPMENT • DOI: 10.1002/cd

Escobar, J., Waitzkin, H., Silver, R., Gara, M., & Holman, A. (1998). Abridged somatization: A study in primary care. *Psychosomatic Medicine, 60,* 466–472.

Fix, M., & Passel, J. (1999, March). *Trends in noncitizens' and citizens' use of public benefits following welfare reform.* Washington, DC: The Urban Institute.

Gundersen, C., & Gruber, J. (2001). *The dynamic determinants of food insufficiency* (Food Assistance and Nutrition Research Report Number 11–2, pp. 91–109). Washington, DC: U.S. Department of Agriculture, Economic Research Service.

Gundersen, C., & Oliveira, V. (2001). The Food Stamps program and food insufficiency. *American Journal of Agricultural Economics, 83,* 875–887.

Hernandez, D. (2004). Demographic change and the life circumstances of immigrant families. *The Future of Children, 14,* 17–47.

Huang, Z., Yu, S., & Ledsky, R. (2006). Health status and health services access and use among children in U.S. immigrant families. *American Journal of Public Health, 96,* 634–640.

Kasper, J., Gupta, S., Tran, P., Cook, J., & Meyers, A. (2000). Hunger in legal immigrants in California, Texas, and Illinois. *American Journal of Public Health, 90,* 1629–1633.

Lara, M., Gamboa, C., Kahramanian, M., Morales, L., & Bautista, D. (2005). Acculturation and Latino health in the United States: A review of the literature and its sociopolitical context. *Annual Review of Public Health, 26,* 367–397.

Martin, K., Rogers, B., Cook, J., & Joseph, H. (2004). Social capital is associated with decreased risk of hunger. *Social Science and Medicine, 58,* 2645–2654.

Nord, M., Andrews, M., & Carlson, S. (2003). *Household food security in the United States, 2002* (Food Assistance and Nutrition Research Report No. 35). Washington, DC: U.S. Department of Agriculture, Food and Rural Economics Division, Economic Research Service.

Nord, M., & Bickel, G. (2002). *Measuring children's food security in U.S. households, 1995–99* (Food Assistance and Nutrition Research Report Number 25). Washington, DC: U.S. Department of Agriculture, Economic Research Service.

Personal Responsibility and Work Opportunity Reconciliation Act, Pub. L. 104–193, 104th Cong. (1996).

Shields, M. K., & Behrman, R. E. (2004). Children of immigrant families: Analysis and recommendations for children of immigrant families. *The Future of Children, 14(2),* 4–16.

Slack, K., & Yoo, J. (2005). Food hardships and child behavior problems among low-income children. *Social Service Review, 79,* 511–536.

Van Hook, J., & Balistreri, K. (2006). Ineligible parents, eligible children: Food Stamps receipt, allotments, and food insecurity among children of immigrants. *Social Science Research, 35,* 228–251.

Wilde, P., & Nord, M. (2005). The effect of Food Stamps on food security: A panel data approach. *Review of Agricultural Economics, 27,* 425–432.

Winicki, J., & Jemison, K. (2003). Food insecurity and hunger in the kindergarten classroom: Its effect on learning and growth. *Contemporary Economic Policy, 21,* 145–157.

Yu, S., Huang, Z., Schwalberg, R., & Kogan, M. (2005). Parental awareness of health and community resources among immigrant families. *Maternal and Child Health Journal, 9,* 27–34.

ARIEL KALIL is Associate Professor of Public Policy at The Harris School of Public Policy at the University of Chicago, IL.

JEN-HAO CHEN is a PhD student at The Harris School of Public Policy at the University of Chicago, IL.

Yoshikawa, H., Godfrey, E. B., & Rivera, A. C. (2008). Access to institutional resources as a measure of social exclusion: Relations with family process and cognitive development in the context of immigration. In H. Yoshikawa & N. Way (Eds.), Beyond the family: Contexts of immigrant children's development. *New Directions for Child and Adolescent Development, 121,* 63–86.

5

Access to Institutional Resources as a Measure of Social Exclusion: Relations With Family Process and Cognitive Development in the Context of Immigration

Hirokazu Yoshikawa, Erin B. Godfrey, Ann C. Rivera

Abstract

Few studies have examined how experiences associated with being an undocumented immigrant parent affects children's development. In this article, the authors apply social exclusion theory to examine how access to institutional resources that require identification may matter for parents and children in immigrant families. As hypothesized, groups with higher proportions of undocumented parents in New York City (e.g., Mexicans compared to Dominicans) reported lower levels of access to checking accounts, savings accounts, credit, and drivers' licenses. Lack of access to such resources, in turn, was associated with higher economic hardship and psychological distress among parents, and lower levels of cognitive ability in their 24-month-old children. © Wiley Periodicals, Inc.

NEW DIRECTIONS FOR CHILD AND ADOLESCENT DEVELOPMENT, no. 121, Fall 2008 © Wiley Periodicals, Inc.
Published online in Wiley InterScience (www.interscience.wiley.com) • DOI: 10.1002/cd.223

63

Little information exists about the developmental status of young children of lower-income immigrants in the United States, despite the fact that children of immigrants are overrepresented among families in and near poverty (Capps, Fix, Ost, Reardon-Anderson, & Passel, 2005). Recent data suggest that some groups are at particular risk. Young children (from newborn to 5 years of age) of immigrants from Mexico, Central America, and the Dominican Republic, for example, are particularly disadvantaged, relative to both other immigrant children and native-born White children, on dimensions of family income, poverty status, parental employment, and parental education (Hernandez, Denton, & McCartney, in press). These all constitute developmental risks for lower levels of health, cognitive ability, and socioemotional competence (Card, 1999; Fuligni & Yoshikawa, 2003; Yeung, Linver, & Brooks-Gunn, 2002). Research conducted with the Early Childhood Longitudinal Study-Kindergarten cohort (ECLS-K) shows that Mexican immigrant parents' relatively low levels of human capital and income appear to only partially explain their children's lower first-grade reading and math scores in comparison to native-born White children (Han, 2006). Other studies show similar results (e.g., Nord & Griffin, 1999).

We posit in this study that social exclusion is a neglected dimension of the experience of some immigrants that may affect family processes and child development, and one that may help explain disparities in cognitive development among different immigrant and native-born groups in the United States. Social exclusion is a major focus of work on disadvantage among immigrants conducted by policy makers and researchers in Europe (Alba, 2005; Burchardt, Le Grand, & Piachaud, 2002; Centre for the Analysis of Social Exclusion, 2005; Glass, 1999; Lenoir, 1974; Saraceno, 2002). The concept of social exclusion was developed to capture dimensions of the experience of immigrants that go beyond poverty to issues of lack of access to political, social, and health systems. Exclusion can occur with reference to public institutions, such as government policies and service systems, as well as social institutions, such as social networks or community organizations. Some have observed that the concept of social exclusion may be useful in the United States as a way to broaden debates beyond poverty as the major source of disadvantage that affects children's prospects (Micklewright, 2002). However, social exclusion has rarely been investigated with relevance to the development of children in the United States, let alone children of immigrants to the United States (Kamerman & Kahn, 2003).

Social exclusion may be particularly relevant for undocumented immigrant parents in the United States. This group is excluded from eligibility from many public institutions and policies, and due to fear of deportation may exclude themselves from others for which they are eligible. Almost no studies have examined the consequences for family process and child development of undocumented status among parents. This is because few developmental researchers ask parents their legal status for ethical and confidentiality reasons. Social exclusion may provide a theoretical lens through which experiences associated with undocumented status can be studied. Although formal policy exclusion (e.g., ineligibility for benefits) has been examined most often with regard to immigrants (e.g., Capps et al., 2005; Yoshikawa, Lugo-Gil, Chaudry, & Tamis-LeMonda, 2005), other dimensions of social exclusion may be salient for this group.

Access to Institutional Resources That Require or Provide Identification: A Dimension of Social Exclusion

It has been observed anecdotally that many undocumented immigrants are reluctant to engage with institutions that require or provide identification. This is due to fears of deportation and uncertainty about the consequences of engaging governmental or other institutions, fears which have heightened in recent years (James, 2005). In this study, we examine access to such institutional resources—drivers' licenses, savings or checking accounts, and financial credit—as aspects of low-income immigrant parents' experience that may have consequences for their economic hardship or psychological well-being. We chose these particular resources because they are obtained through contact with financial and government institutions that require forms of identification, and may therefore be shunned by undocumented parents.

One salient dimension of social exclusion among low-income immigrant parents may be access to and use of institutions that require or provide formal identification. Banks are one example of such institutions; government institutions such as departments of motor vehicles, which issue drivers' licenses, are another. Access to such institutions and their services, we argue, may be related to both economic and psychological well-being among parents. For example, having a checking or savings account can result in higher assets. Higher household assets, in turn, have been associated with long-term benefits for the life course including higher educational success and attainment among children in the household (Conley, 1999). The benefits of savings behavior for households in poverty are the basis for efforts to increase savings behavior such as Individual Development Account (IDA) programs (Grinstein-Weiss, Wagner, & Ssewamala, 2006; Sherraden, 1991).

Policies about documents required to obtain a driver's license, the most common form of identification in the United States, vary from state to state. Several states have recently made it more difficult for undocumented immigrants to obtain drivers' licenses (Preston, 2007). In New York State, the state of residence for all of the parents in the current sample, a social security card is required, or proof of reason for ineligibility for a social security card. That proof must be provided in the form of a document from the federal Citizenship and Immigration Services (USCIS). It is likely that undocumented parents do not wish to provide such documentation to obtain a drivers' license.

NEW DIRECTIONS FOR CHILD AND ADOLESCENT DEVELOPMENT • DOI: 10.1002/cd

We hypothesize that levels of access to these resources may vary across ethnic and immigrant groups that differ in likelihood of being undocumented (our three groups of interest are low-income Mexican and Dominican immigrant parents, and low-income, U.S.-born African American parents—all from New York City). Among the three groups, we hypothesize that African American parents will have the highest levels of access to our focal institutions because they are all U.S. citizens by virtue of being born in the country. Among our two Latino immigrant groups, Mexicans are more likely to be undocumented; this is a very recent immigrant group to the New York City area, and one with relatively low levels of human capital and less-developed social networks than the Dominicans, who have been emigrating to New York for several decades (Pessar & Graham, 2002; Smith, 2006).

Access to Institutional Resources: Links to Family Processes and Child Development

We also hypothesize in this study that access to institutional resources may affect family processes and children's early cognitive development. We explore three potential mediators of the associations of access with child cognitive development: economic hardship, psychological distress, and cognitive stimulation.

Having access to checking and savings accounts or credit may in the short run be associated with lower economic hardship and higher levels of resources in the family for children. This is because such financial services can provide a "cushion" in times of particular financial need, and therefore mitigate fluctuations in economic stress in the household (Barr, 2004). In addition, such access may reduce worry and psychological distress among parents. A recent study found that higher economic resources in the household were indeed associated with both lower perceived economic hardship and psychological distress among low-income parents (Mistry, Vandewater, Huston, & McLoyd, 2002). Driver's licenses are a commonly requested form of identification for a wide range of resources and jobs. Having access to a driver's license may therefore also be associated with lower economic and psychological distress.

Economic hardship and psychological distress among parents are, in turn, associated with lower levels of cognitive development in children in many studies (e.g., Gershoff, Aber, Raver, & Lennon, 2007; Jackson, Brooks-Gunn, Huang, & Glassman, 2000; McLoyd, 1990; Mistry et al., 2002; for a review see McLoyd, 1998). Several of these studies show that these factors are associated with less optimal parenting interactions with children, and that these features of parenting may explain effects on children. For example, hardship and distress are both associated with lower levels of cognitive stimulation of children, which, in turn, is associated with lower levels of children's early receptive and productive vocabulary as well as more general cognitive development (Bradley, Corwyn, Burchinal, McAdoo, & Garcia Coll, 2001; Gershoff et al., 2007).

Current Study

The research questions and hypotheses for this study are (a) What levels of access to institutional resources are reported by low-income immigrant and ethnically diverse parents? (b) Is more access to institutional resources related to lower levels of economic hardship and psychological distress, and higher levels of parent cognitive stimulation? (c) Are hardship, distress, and stimulation, in turn, related to indicators of children's early cognitive ability?

We hypothesize that, in our urban, low-income sample, U.S.-born African Americans will report the highest levels of such access, followed by Dominicans and then by Mexicans. We also hypothesize that economic hardship and psychological distress are related to lower levels of cognitive ability, and that cognitive stimulation is related to higher levels of cognitive ability.

The conceptual models for this study (Figures 5.1 and 5.2) link access to institutional resources that require or provide identification to children's early cognitive and socioemotional development, as mediated by material hardship, psychological distress, and parent engagement in cognitively stimulating learning activities. Figure 5.1 depicts the estimates of differences among all three ethnic groups, with dummy variables for Mexican and Dominican (African American as reference group). Figure 5.2 shows the differences between the two Latino groups (dummy variable for Mexican, with Dominican as the reference group).

Method

Data for this study came from an ongoing longitudinal study investigating the lives of low-income and immigrant mothers and their newborn children, the Early Childhood Cohort (ECC) of the Center for Research on Culture, Development and Education (CRCDE). Researchers recruited mothers within 2 days after giving birth at postpartum wards in three large New York City hospitals during 2004–2005. These hospitals were selected because they drew patients from low-income neighborhoods with high concentrations of the four target ethnic groups. To participate in the study, mothers had to be over age 18, live in New York City, self-identify as Chinese, Mexican, Dominican, or African American, and have healthy fullterm infants. These ethnic groups were targeted for the study because together they represent over 80% of the population of New York City and include the largest immigrant groups in the city. The initial sample was comprised of 382 mothers recruited from hospital maternity wards shortly after giving birth. Chinese participants were dropped from the study after the 6-month wave because a high number of them sent their infants to China to be raised by relatives. The initial sample of Dominican, Mexican, and African American mothers consisted of 324.

For the current study, the sample is limited to Dominican, Mexican, and African American mothers who completed the 24-month wave of data

NEW DIRECTIONS FOR CHILD AND ADOLESCENT DEVELOPMENT • DOI: 10.1002/cd

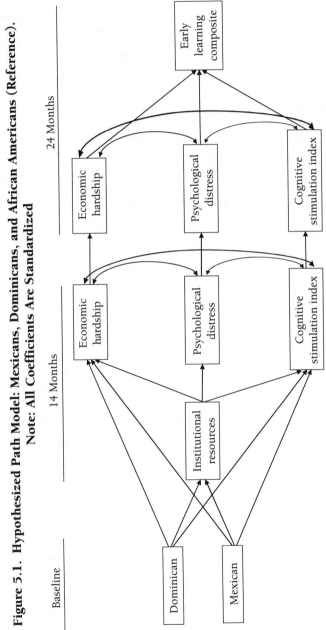

Figure 5.1. Hypothesized Path Model: Mexicans, Dominicans, and African Americans (Reference).
Note: All Coefficients Are Standardized

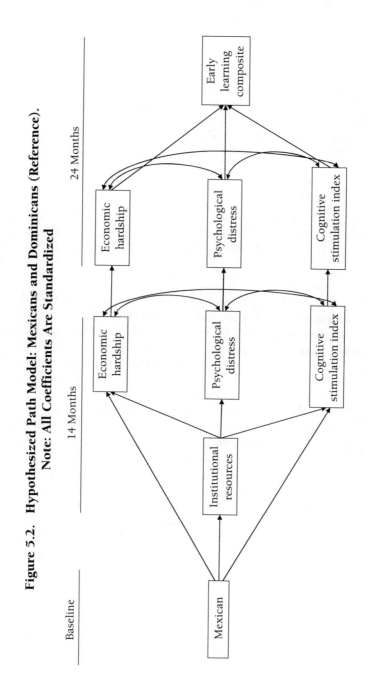

**Figure 5.2. Hypothesized Path Model: Mexicans and Dominicans (Reference).
Note: All Coefficients Are Standardized**

Table 5.1. Participant Characteristics at Baseline: Survey Sample at 24-Month Follow-Up

	Full Sample (n = 181)	Mexicans (n = 62)	Dominicans (n = 64)	African Americans (n = 55)
Percentage				
Mother under 18 when 1st child born	13%	13%	10%	18%
Mother married or cohabiting with partner	67%	85%	61%	53%
Mother has HS degree	37%	40%	31%	40%
Mean (SD)				
Total number of children in household	2.05 (1.19)	2.00 (1.17)	1.73 (0.84)	2.27 (1.84)
Household income in year prior to child's birth	$20,206 ($14,423)	$17,498 ($11,536)	$23,192 ($15,086)	$19,983 ($16,436)

collection (N = 198). Eighty percent of Dominican mothers and 95% of Mexican mothers were foreign-born; all African American mothers were native-born. We conducted an attrition analysis using a set of baseline covariates to predict nonparticipation at the 24-month wave. Fourteen demographic variables served as predictors in this analysis: racial/ethnic group, maternal age, teen motherhood, maternal and paternal immigrant status, maternal–paternal marital status, maternal cohabiting status, mother has high school degree, mother has higher degree, maternal employment in the prior year, mothers' earnings in the prior year, child age at recruitment, and child gender. Of these, only mother has high school degree was a significant predictor of attrition, $b = -1.00$ (.35), $p = .005$, OR = .37, indicating that mothers with a high school degree were significantly less likely to drop out than mothers without a high school degree. Select demographic characteristics of the sample are listed in Table 5.1.

Data used in this study were obtained from assessments at baseline, 14, and 24 months. Trained, bilingual researchers recruited families individually at hospitals shortly after the birth of their children, explaining that the study aimed to learn more about children's early years and about parents' experiences raising their children. After acquiring parents' consent, researchers conducted baseline survey interviews of 30- to 40-minutes duration. When infants were 14 months old, researchers interviewed mothers face-to-face in their homes and completed direct assessments of children's cognitive development.[1] At the 24-month data assessment, survey instruments were

[1]For mothers who preferred to be interviewed away from their homes, researchers completed interviews and assessments in a private location on the university's campus.

again administered in person through interview format and a child cognitive assessment was also completed. Trained, bilingual female graduate students collected all data in the mother's preferred language (English or Spanish). Participants were compensated $25 for the baseline interview, $50 for the 14-month interview/home visit, and $75 for the 24-month interview/home visit. The institutional review boards at New York University and the three recruitment hospitals approved all study procedures.

Baseline Covariates. Measures collected at the baseline interview include whether the mother has a high school education (dummy variable); the household's income in the year prior to the child's birth; and whether the father of the child and/or a partner coresided in the mother's home (dummy variable).

Access to Institutional Resources. Household access to institutional resources was assessed through a 4-item index at the 14-month wave. Mothers were asked to indicate (yes/no) whether they or anyone in their household has (a) a checking account, (b) a savings account, (c) a credit card, and (d) a driver's license. These items were then summed to create an index of household access to institutional resources ($M = 2.00$, $SD = 1.50$, range: 0–4).

Economic Hardship. Economic hardship was measured at both the 14- and 24-month waves using a 4-item index assessing whether there has been a time in the past 6 months (yes/no) when they and their family (a) were without telephone service; (b) did not pay the full amount of the rent or mortgage; (c) were evicted from their home or apartment for not paying the rent or mortgage; or (d) lost service from the gas, electric, or oil companies because payments were not made. These items were then summed to create an index of economic hardship (14-month wave: $M = 0.49$, $SD = 0.75$, range: 0–3; 24-month wave: $M = 0.33$, $SD = 0.61$, range: 0–3).

Psychological Distress. Psychological distress was measured at both the 14- and 24-month waves using the K6 (Kessler et al., 2002), a 6-item diagnostic scale measuring general psychological distress including depressive and anxious affect ($\alpha = .80$). Mothers were asked to report on the frequency of feelings of distress in the past 30 days on a 5-point scale ranging from 1 (*none of the time*) to 5 (*all of the time*). Sample items include "During the past 30 days how often did you feel hopeless?" and "About how often in the past 30 days have you felt nervous?" The sample mean of psychological distress is 1.89 ($SD = 0.72$) at the 14-month wave and 1.81 ($SD = 0.70$) at the 24-month wave.

Daily Cognitive Stimulation. Mothers' reports of activities with their child were used to create an index of six cognitively stimulating activities at both the 14- and 24-month waves, including singing songs, reading/looking at books, telling stories, listening or dancing to music, playing games that do not involve toys, and playing with building toys. These include activities that have been reported with moderate frequency among Mexican American and other Latino mothers in the United States (Delgado-Gaitan, 1990; Hammer

& Miccio, 2004). To reduce the possibility of bias due to social desirability, mothers who reported engaging with their child every day in each activity were given a one, those who reported anything less were given a zero. (In a national low-income sample with children of this age, a recent study has found stronger sequelae for later cognitive development of mothers' reports of reading daily when compared to less frequent reading; Raikes et al., 2006.) The six items were then summed to create an index of cognitive stimulation (14-month wave: $M = 2.65$, $SD = 1.39$, range: 0–6; 24-month wave: $M = 2.08$, $SD = 1.40$, range: 0–6).

Child Cognitive Development. The Mullen Scales of Early Learning (MSEL; Mullen, 1995) were used to capture children's cognitive development at the 24-month wave. The MSEL, an interviewer-administered standardized developmental test for children aged 3–60 months, consists of four subscales of cognitive development: visual reception, fine motor skills, receptive language, and expressive language. Scores on each subscale are age-equivalent normed and can be combined to provide an index of overall developmental level, the Early Learning Composite. We report results for both the overall Early Learning Composite and each subscale below. Subscales have a mean of 50 and a standard deviation of 10; the early learning composite has a mean of 100 and a standard deviation of 15. The MSEL correlates highly with other measures of cognitive development in early childhood, including the Bayley Scales of Infant Development (Mullen, 1995). Sample means for each of the scales are 43.4 ($SD = 9.8$) for visual reception; 37.8 ($SD = 12.2$) for fine motor skills; 44.9 ($SD = 9.4$) for receptive language; 37.7 ($SD = 8.0$) for expressive language; and 83.3 ($SD = 13.7$) for the early learning composite.

Results

Structural equation modeling techniques were used to estimate a path model representing the hypothesized set of relationships between institutional exclusion, economic hardship and parenting, and child cognitive development. Structural equation modeling is more flexible in its statistical assumptions than regression, provides indicators of overall model fit, and has the ability to simultaneously estimate paths. Therefore, it is a useful tool for exploring multiple relationships at the same time and is often used to reduce bias in mediation analyses (Kline, 1998; Shrout & Bolger, 2002).

Two a priori path models were conceptualized, one in which African American mothers served as the reference group (see Figure 5.1) and one in which the sample was limited to Mexican and Dominican mothers and Dominican mothers served as the reference group (see Figure 5.2). The first model allows us to examine the hypothesized differences in access to institutional resources between the two immigrant groups (Mexicans and Dominicans) and the U.S.-born group (African Americans). The second model examines the hypothesized difference between the Mexicans and Dominicans. In both models, we included the hardship, distress, and stimulation constructs at two waves of measurement: 14 months and 24 months.

Both models were estimated using the sample covariance matrix and maximum likelihood estimation. Full information maximum likelihood was used using the Amos 6.0 statistical package to model and estimate all parameters (Arbuckle, 2005). Amos uses full information maximum likelihood estimates in the presence of missing data, a strategy that yields efficient and consistent estimates in the presence of data that are either missing completely at random or missing at random and produces least biased estimates in the case of non-ignorable missing data (Schafer & Graham, 2002).

As recommended by Hu and Bentler (1995) and Kline (1998), models were evaluated using several indices of overall fit. These include the comparative fit index (CFI; adequate fit >.90), the non-normed fit index (NNFI; adequate fit >.90), and the root-mean-square-error of approximation (RMSEA; adequate fit <.05). We also report 90% confidence intervals (CI) for the RMSEA statistic. In addition, as recommended by Kline (1998), the residual correlation matrices were inspected for residuals over .10, which indicate a poorer fit for that portion of the model. Although the overall chi square is reported in this paper, it is only used to create the chi square difference test which compares the fit of one model to a nested model.[2] Direct paths between the baseline covariates and both the principal predictor (institutional resources) and child outcomes were estimated, along with covariances among the covariates and between each covariate and racial/ethnic group membership. Comparisons of models with and without additional covariates (including employment, number of children in household, and child gender) indicated few differences in obtained path coefficients; for reasons of statistical power, analyses with the reduced set of covariates are reported.

As suggested when testing structural equation models (Kline, 1998), alternative models were also examined. Analyses began by estimating the hypothesized models presented in Figures 5.1 and 5.2 and examining the fit statistics, residual correlation matrices, and measurement equations. The hypothesized models were then trimmed on both theoretical and empirical grounds and the $\chi^2\Delta$ statistic was used to evaluate changes in model fit.

The finalized path model for our institutional resource model with the full sample of Mexicans, Dominicans, and African Americans is presented in Figure 5.3. In this analysis, African American mothers served as the reference group. The model was overidentified with degrees of freedom $(df)= 51$ and fit statistics indicated a good fit for the data: $\chi^2(51) = 58.86$, NNFI = 0.97, CFI = 0.98, RMSEA = .022 (90% CI = .000–.043). Mexican mothers reported lower access to institutional resources, $b = -.69$ (0.25), $p < .01$, $\beta = -0.21$, and lower economic hardship, $b = -.33$ (0.13), $p = .01$, $\beta = -0.20$, than African American mothers. In addition, Dominican mothers

---

[2]The χ^2 test evaluates whether the fit of the simplified model is different from the fit of the saturated model. It is not often used as a fit measure because of its dependence on sample size.

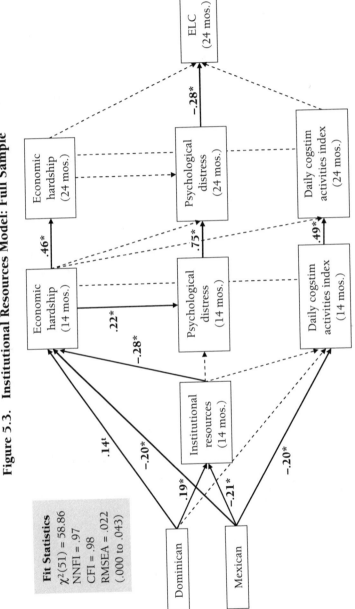

Figure 5.3. Institutional Resources Model: Full Sample

Fit Statistics
$\chi^2(51) = 58.86$
NNFI = .97
CFI = .98
RMSEA = .022
(.000 to .043)

Note: Paths in bold are statistically significant
Numbers in diagram are standardized path coefficients
Covariates include: mom has HS degree; mom cohabiting w/partner; hhld income in prior yr
Model estimated: all covariances between exogenous variables and direct paths between covariates, institutional resources, and child outcomes

reported significantly higher access to institutional resources, $b = .60$ (0.23), $p < .05$, $\beta = -0.19$, and higher economic hardship, $b = 0.21$ (0.12), $p < .10$, $\beta = 0.14$, than African American mothers, although the difference for hardship was of marginal significance. Mexican mothers also reported fewer daily cognitively stimulating activities, $b = -.62$ (0.25), $p < .05$, $\beta = -0.20$, than their African American counterparts. Higher access to institutional resources, in turn, predicted lower levels of economic hardship, $b = -0.14$ (0.04), $p < .001$, $\beta = -0.28$, and lower economic hardship was related to lower psychological distress, $b = 0.20$ (0.07), $p < .01$, $\beta = 0.22$. We found moderate to high stability in our mediator constructs, with standardized coefficients of .46, .75, and .49 for economic hardship, psychological distress, and cognitive stimulation, respectively (all significant at the .05 level).

Finally, psychological distress was associated with lower scores on the Mullen Early Learning Composite, $b = -5.55$ (1.48), $p < .001$, $\beta = -0.28$. In the subscale-specific analyses (available from the authors), psychological distress was negatively related to visual reception ($b = -2.09$ (1.04), $p < .05$; $\beta = -0.15$, fine motor skills, $b = -2.93$ (1.31), $p < .05$, $\beta = -0.17$, receptive language, $b = -2.16$ (1.03), $p < .05$; $\beta = -0.16$, and expressive language, $b = -2.56$ (0.88), $p < .01$, $\beta = -0.22$. In addition, a significant negative association was found for economic hardship with visual reception, $b = -2.32$ (1.19), $p < .05$, $\beta = -0.14$.

The finalized path model for Mexicans and Dominicans is presented in Figure 5.4. In this analysis, Dominican mothers now served as the reference group. This model was also overidentified ($df = 43$), and fit statistics indicated an adequate fit for the data: χ^2 (43) = 29.10, NNFI = 1.12, CFI = 1.00, RMSEA = .000 (CI = .000 to .004). Fit statistics were somewhat better for this model without covariates, but we report the model with covariates; there was little substantive difference in the pattern or magnitude of path coefficients. In this model, Mexican mothers reported lower access to institutional resources than Dominican mothers, $b = -1.25$ (0.25), $p < .001$, $\beta = -0.41$, as well as lower economic hardship, $b = -0.55$ (0.14), $p < .001$, $\beta = -0.37$. Higher access to institutional resources again predicted lower reports of economic hardship, $b = -0.14$ (0.05), $p < .01$, $\beta = -0.30$, and lower economic hardship was related to lower psychological distress, $b = 0.18$ (0.08), $p < .05$, $\beta = 0.18$. Compared to the model with the full sample, the relationship between psychological distress and child cognitive development was in the same direction and of similar magnitude, $b = -4.62$ (1.61), $p < .01$, $\beta = -0.25$. In the subscale-specific analyses, more psychological distress predicted lower scores on all subscales of the MSEL except for receptive language: visual reception, $b = -2.09$ (1.04); $p < .05$, $\beta = -0.19$, fine motor skills, $b = -2.93$ (1.31), $p < .05$, $\beta = -0.22$, and expressive language, $b = -2.56$ (0.88), $p < .01$, $\beta = -0.16$. In this analysis, the association between economic hardship and the visual reception subscale was no longer significant. However, daily cognitively stimulating activities did predict higher scores on the visual reception scale, $b = 0.21$ (0.10), $p < .05$, $\beta = 0.18$.

Figure 5.4. Institutional Resources Models: Mexicans and Dominicans

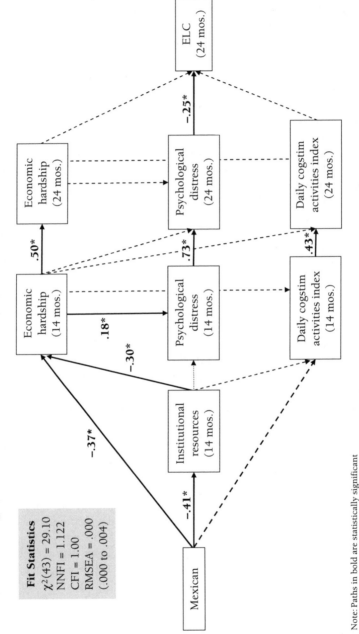

Fit Statistics
$\chi^2(43) = 29.10$
NNFI = 1.122
CFI = 1.00
RMSEA = .000
(.000 to .004)

Note: Paths in bold are statistically significant
Numbers in diagram are standardized path coefficients
Covariates include: mom has HS degree; mom cohabiting w/partner; hhld income in prior yr
Model estimated: all covariances between exogenous variables and direct paths between covariates, institutional resources and child outcomes

Due to the policy relevance of access to driver's licenses, we examined the models with just that item, separate from the savings, checking, and credit items. These models are presented in Figures 5.5 and 5.6. In the finalized path model for our driver's license model with the full sample of Mexicans, Dominicans, and African Americans (Figure 5.5), African American mothers served as the reference group. The model was overidentified with $df = 51$, and fit statistics indicated a good fit for the data: $\chi^2(51) = 62.06$, NNFI = 0.95, CFI = 0.97, RMSEA = .026, 90% CI = .000–046. The paths between mother's ethnicity and the mediators were the same, except that the difference between Dominican and African American mothers' reports of economic hardship was no longer significant. In this model, access to a driver's license again predicted lower reports of economic hardship, but only at a marginal significance level, $b = -0.21 (0.12)$, $p < .10$, $\beta = -0.14$, and economic hardship again predicted psychological distress, $b = 0.20 (0.07)$, $p < .01$, $\beta = 0.22$. As in the institutional resources model with the full sample, psychological distress predicted child cognitive development (standardized coefficient of $-.28$). In the subscale-specific analyses, the paths between psychological distress and all four scales of the MSEL were in the same direction and of similar magnitude compared to the institutional resources model; higher psychological distress predicted lower scores on the visual reception, $b = -2.09 (1.04)$, $p < .05$, $\beta = -0.15$, fine motor skills, $b = -2.93$ (1.31), $p < .05$, $\beta = -0.16$, receptive language, $b = -2.16 (1.03)$, $p < .05$, $\beta = -0.16$, and expressive language, $b = -2.55 (0.88)$, $p < .01$, $\beta = -0.22$, subscales of the MSEL. The path between economic hardship and the visual reception subscale was also similar in magnitude, when compared to the institutional resources model, $b = -2.32 (1.19)$, $p = .05$, $\beta = -0.14$.

In the finalized driver's license model with the Mexicans and Dominicans (Figure 5.6), Dominican mothers served as the reference group. The model was overidentified with $df = 43$, and fit statistics indicated a good fit for the data: $\chi^2(43) = 38.82$, NNFI = 1.04, CFI = 1.00, RMSEA = .000, 90% CI = .000–.032. As in the institutional resources model with the reduced sample, economic hardship predicted psychological distress at a marginally significant level, $b = 0.15 (0.08)$, $p < .10$, $\beta = 0.16$, and distress significantly predicted child cognitive development, $b = -4.61 (1.61)$, $p < .01$, $\beta = -0.25$. In the subscale-specific analyses, the paths between psychological distress and the subscales of the MSEL were in the same direction and of similar magnitude as in the institutional resources model with the equivalent sample. Again, the path coefficient between daily cognitively stimulating activities and the visual reception scale of the MSEL was significant, $b = 1.04 (0.58)$, $p < .10$, $\beta = 0.16$, though at a marginal level of significance.

Finally, a multisample path analysis was run to evaluate whether the relationships between the endogenous variables in the model differed by racial/ethnic group. In this analysis, racial/ethnic group was no longer used to predict the system of relationships. Instead, the system of relationships was

NEW DIRECTIONS FOR CHILD AND ADOLESCENT DEVELOPMENT • DOI: 10.1002/cd

Figure 5.5. Driver's License Model: Full Sample

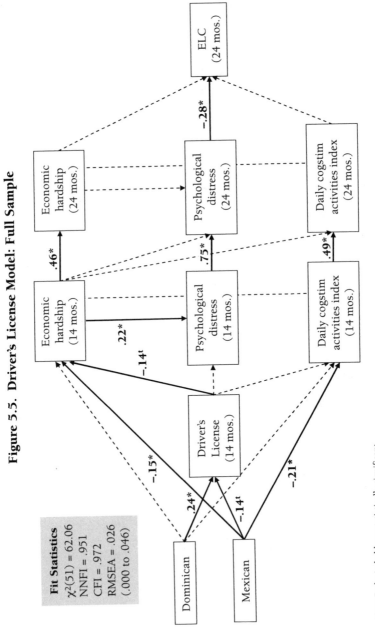

Fit Statistics
$\chi^2(51) = 62.06$
NNFI = .951
CFI = .972
RMSEA = .026
(.000 to .046)

Note: Paths in bold are statistically significant
Numbers in diagram are standardized path coefficients
Covariates include: mom has HS degree; mom cohabiting w/partner; hhld income in prior yr
Model estimated: all covariances between exogenous variables and direct paths between covariates, institutional resources and child outcomes

Figure 5.6. Driver's License Model: Mexicans and Dominicans

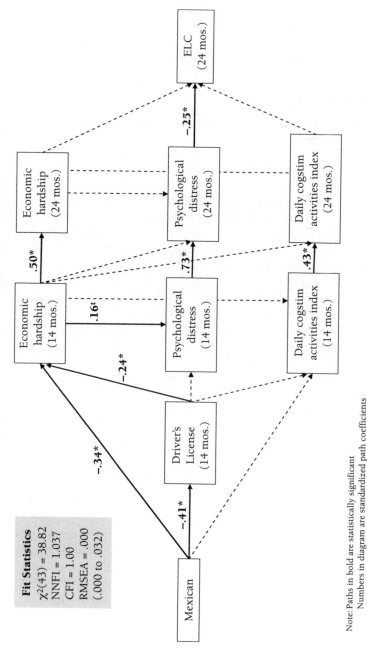

Fit Statistics
$\chi^2(43) = 38.82$
NNFI = 1.037
CFI = 1.00
RMSEA = .000
(.000 to .032)

Note: Paths in bold are statistically significant
Numbers in diagram are standardized path coefficients
Covariates include: mom has HS degree; mom cohabiting w/partner; hhld income in prior yr
Model estimated: all covariances between exogenous variables and direct paths between covariates, institutional resources and child outcomes

compared across the Mexican, Dominican, and African American samples to determine whether the structural paths differed or remained the same across groups. A model in which all parameters was allowed to vary across groups was compared to models in which parameters were constrained to be equal across. Both the overall fit indices and $\chi^2\Delta$ statistics for these models indicated that the relationships between variables do not vary across racial/ethnic group.

Discussion

This study aimed to explore implications of social exclusion theory for the experience of low-income immigrant parents with young children in the United States. Social exclusion is a construct applied (primarily in work outside the United States) to capture dimensions of disadvantage that standard economic constructs such as poverty or hardship do not capture (Burchardt et al., 2002). We applied social exclusion theory to the experiences of exclusion that might be related to undocumented status among low-income immigrants. Few studies have explored the ramifications for children of parents' undocumented status, because of difficulty in directly assessing legal status. Social exclusion provides a theory that can help us pinpoint the multiple experiences associated with this status.

Specifically, this study is the first to link institutional dimensions of social exclusion among immigrant parents to their family processes and children's development. We posited that low-income immigrant parents, due in part to variation in their legal status, might vary in their likelihood to access resources that require them to show identification. Thus, we sought to explore institutional access as one indicator of social exclusion that goes beyond the usual poverty-based definitions of exclusion.

In our models, we examined how access to institutions that require forms of identification (savings accounts and checking accounts, credit cards, and driver's licenses) related to economic hardship, psychological distress, and cognitive stimulation of children. We further examined how these three factors were related to a standardized assessment of children's cognitive abilities at 24 months.

In brief, our findings supported much of our theoretical model linking institutional access to children's development through our hypothesized mediators. Household-level access to institutional resources was associated with lower economic hardship, which, in turn, was associated with higher psychological distress over time and lower levels of cognitive ability (see Figure 5.3). We had hypothesized that having access to checking or savings accounts and credit might provide a financial cushion during times of economic hardship. This appears to be reflected in our data, with a moderate negative relationship (standardized coefficient of −.28; Figure 5.3) between access to institutional resources and economic hardship (as represented by items such as having phone service cut off or not being able to meet bill deadlines). We also hypothesized that the process of saving for the future, together with the higher economic resources such savings bring, would predict higher levels of resource-dependent investments in children, such as reading books for children or other forms of cognitive stimulation. This part of the model, however, was not supported.

Mexicans consistently reported lower levels of daily cognitive stimulation with their children than Dominicans or African Americans; however, the measure of daily cognitive stimulation was not associated with the total score on our cognitive assessment.

In analyses separating our standardized assessment into its four component subscales (visual reception, fine motor skills, expressive language, and receptive language) we found some different patterns, depending on the particular predictor being examined. Economic hardship appeared to be most strongly related to visual reception, and less so to the other subscales. Psychological distress was related to all four subscales in the predicted direction (higher distress associated with lower levels of the particular ability). Finally, daily cognitive stimulation was related to higher visual perception, but not the other subscales. These differences are somewhat difficult to interpret, partly because the cognitive measure is taken quite early in early childhood (in the midst of the first vocabulary "spurt" that children experience), with still a bit of "noise" in these subscale measures. This is reflected in the fact that the associations of distress with these subscales were quite a bit weaker (standardized coefficients ranging from $-.15$ to $-.22$) than with the entire scale as a whole (standardized coefficient of $-.28$).

We were also interested in variation among our sample of Mexicans, Dominicans, and African Americans in institutional resources and the other constructs in our model. Although our groups were fairly similar in class (all being of low incomes), they varied in degree of political incorporation. The Mexican mothers were all first generation; about 80% of the Dominicans were first generation. These differences, together with the fact that the Mexican group were by far the lowest in terms of parental human capital and income, drove our hypotheses that the Mexicans were likely to have the highest proportion of undocumented parents, followed by the Dominicans, and then of course no parents of undocumented status among the African Americans. We therefore predicted that the Mexicans would report the lowest levels of institutional resources, followed by the Dominicans and then the African Americans. This hypothesis was only partially supported. That is, Dominican parents reported higher levels of household access to these resources than African American parents. Mexicans, as hypothesized, did report the lowest levels of these resources.

Why did Dominican parents report higher levels of financial banking resources and driver's licenses than African American parents? One reason may be the higher rates of young motherhood and single parenthood among the African American parents. This group was more likely to be living with grandmothers. Our qualitative data, for example, suggest that some of the younger African American single mothers in our sample left the financial responsibilities in the household to the grandparents (Lugo-Gil, Yoshikawa, & Tamis-LeMonda, 2006). Another possibility is that the Dominican families may have had more extensive social networks. This possibility is now being explored through data we are collecting on social network size, availability, and support.

We also included paths in our model from ethnic group directly to economic hardship. Here again, we encountered a somewhat counterintuitive finding: The Mexicans reported lower levels of economic hardship than both the African Americans and the Dominicans. This occurred despite their lower incomes and lower levels of human capital. Why did the poorest among our groups report the least hardship? Two principal reasons may explain this puzzling finding. First, as work by the Suárez-Orozcos (Suárez-Orozco, 1989; Suárez-Orozco & Suárez-Orozco, 2001) and others indicates, immigrants often evince a "dual frame of reference" in their experience, one relevant to their context of reception and one relevant to their sending context. Our Mexican sample comes from a particularly poor state in Mexico, Puebla (Yoshikawa et al., 2008). These parents, in our qualitative study, reported more extreme reports of hardship in Puebla than our Dominican parents did when talking about sending contexts in the Dominican Republic. The Mexicans also described government and public support for families in their home country as sparse and unreliable (Yoshikawa et al., 2005). Second, data from some of our other studies suggest that the Mexicans use a variety of survival strategies to live in New York City while managing to make ends meet as well as sending remittances back to Mexico. These include doubling up in apartments (they have higher numbers of people in the home than our Dominicans or African Americans), and participating in informal lending pools (Yoshikawa & Rivera, 2007). These (sometimes called *tanda*) involve regular small deposits to a kitty of money that a group of relatives and friends pitch into, with access to relatively large sums on occasion to take care of big-ticket expenses or debts.

Driver's licenses are currently the focus of much debate and new legislation. Questions being discussed in state legislatures include whether undocumented immigrants should be allowed to have driver's licenses, and what kinds of information (e.g., checks with the federal immigration service or with national terrorist databases) should be required in applications for licenses. We analyzed our models replacing the overall institutional resources measure with the item specific to whether anyone in the household had a driver's license. We found that much of the original model was also supported for the item tapping access to a driver's license in the household. That is, Mexicans reported the lowest likelihood of having a license in the household (Dominicans and African Americans did not significantly differ on this likelihood). Having a driver's license, in turn, was associated with lower perceived economic hardship, which, in turn, related to higher psychological distress and lower scores on the cognitive Mullen assessment.

Several limitations of this study should be noted. First, does institutional access represent a causal influence on parenting and child development, or is it simply a marker of other kinds of disadvantage that undocumented immigrants experience? In our study, due to the lack of a direct measure of legal status, we cannot compare the relative associations of our measure of access with undocumented status itself. Although we controlled for a range of household factors, including prior education, family structure, and income, there exist other family-level factors that might have influenced our results. We did run expanded models with a larger set of covariates, and results were very similar with regard to principal path coefficients, although significance levels were lower. In future work, to address issues of omitted-variables bias, we plan to assess institutional resources again at 36 months. This will allow for individual fixed-effects analyses that predict change in children's outcomes from change in levels of access, an analysis approach that better adjusts for unobserved selection factors that are stable over time and could be responsible for the links between access, family processes, and the child outcomes.

Second, although we began our study with a low-income immigrant Chinese sample in addition to the three groups reported on here, we were unable to continue to follow up that group due to high rates of sending infants back to China. Future work on institutional resources should include this important and largest Asian immigrant group.

Despite these limitations, this study represents a step forward in extending the social science literature on the experience of low-income and undocumented immigrants beyond notions of poverty and economic disadvantage. We believe that studies examining the usual correlates of disadvantage in the United States—income, education, and occupation—do not fully represent the kinds of disadvantage that affect parents' well-being, parenting, and child development in undocumented immigrant families. We demonstrate that institutional access and exclusion, as reflected in this study by household-level access to financial services and drivers' licenses, may be an important, but overlooked influence on family life and child development.

References

Alba, R. (2005). Bright vs. blurred boundaries: Second-generation assimilation and exclusion in France, Germany, and the United States. *Ethnic and Racial Studies, 28,* 20–49.

Arbuckle, J. L. (2005). *Amos 6.0 User's Guide.* Chicago, IL: SPSS.

Barr, M. S. (2004). Banking the poor. *Yale Journal on Regulation, 21,* 121–237.

Bradley, R. H., Corwyn, R. F., Burchinal, M., McAdoo, H., & Garcia Coll, C. (2001). The home environments of children in the United States. Part II: Relations with behavioral development through age thirteen. *Child Development, 72,* 1868–1886.

Burchardt, T., Le Grand, J., & Piachaud, D. (2002). (Eds.). *Understanding social exclusion* (pp. 1–12). Oxford: Oxford University Press.

Capps, R., Fix, M., Ost, J., Reardon-Anderson, J., & Passel, J. (2005). *The health and wellbeing of young children of immigrants.* Washington, DC: The Urban Institute.

Card, D. (1999). The causal effect of education on earnings. In D. T. Mortensen, C. A. Pissarides, O. Ashenfelter, & D. Card (Eds.), *Handbook of labor economics* (Vol. 3, pp. 1801–1863). Amsterdam: North Holland.

Centre for the Analysis of Social Exclusion. (2005). *Annual report: 2004.* London: London School of Economics.

Conley, D. (1999). *Being Black, living in the red: Race, wealth and social policy in America.* Berkeley: University of California Press.

Delgado-Gaitan, C. (1990). *Literacy for empowerment: The role of parents in children's education.* New York: Falmer.

Fuligni, A. J., & Yoshikawa, H. (2003). Socioeconomic resources, parenting, and child development among immigrant families. In M. Bornstein & R. Bradley (Eds.), *Socioeconomic status, parenting, and child development* (pp. 107–124). Mahwah, NJ: Erlbaum.

Gershoff, E. T., Aber, J. L., Raver, C. C., & Lennon, M. C. (2007). Income is not enough: Incorporating material hardship into models of income associations with parent mediators and child outcomes. *Child Development, 78,* 70–95.

Glass, N. (1999). Sure Start: The development of an early intervention programme for young children in the United Kingdom. *Children and Society, 13,* 242–256.

Grinstein-Weiss, M., Wagner, K., & Ssewamala, F. M. (2006). Saving and asset accumulation among low-income families with children in IDA's. *Children and Youth Services Review, 28,* 193–211.

Hammer, C. S., & Miccio, A. W. (2004). Home literacy experiences of Latino families. In B. Wasik (Ed.), *Handbook of family literacy* (pp. 305–328). Mahwah, NJ: Erlbaum.

Han, W. (2006). Academic achievements of children in immigrant families. *Educational Research and Reviews, 1*(8), 286–318.

Hernandez, D., Denton, N. A., & McCartney, S. E. (in press). Early education programs: Differential access among young children in newcomer and native families. In M. Waters & R. Alba (Eds.), *The next generation: Immigrant youth and families in comparative perspective.* Ithaca, NY: Cornell University Press.

Hu, L., & Bentler, P. M. (1995). Evaluating model fit. In R. H. Hoyle (Ed.), *Structural equation modeling: Concepts, issues, and applications* (pp. 76–99). London: Sage.

Jackson, A. P., Brooks-Gunn, J., Huang, C., & Glassman, M. (2000). Single mothers in low-wage jobs: Financial strain, parenting, and preschoolers' outcomes. *Child Development, 71,* 1409–1423.

James, S. D. (2005, June 19). For illegal immigrants, a harsh lesson. *The New York Times,* Section 14NJ, p. 1.

Kamerman, S. B., & Kahn, A. J. (2003). *Beyond child poverty: The social exclusion of children.* Issue Brief of the Clearinghouse on International Developments in Child, Youth, and Family Policies. New York: Columbia University.

Kessler, R. C., Andrews, G., Colpe, L. J., Hiripi, E., Mroczek, D. K., Normand, S.-L. T., et al. (2002). Short screening scales to monitor population prevalences and trends in non-specific psychological distress. *Psychological Medicine, 32,* 959–976.

Kline, R. B. (1998). *Principles and practice of structural equation modeling.* New York: Guilford Press.

Lenoir, R. (1974). *Les Exclus: Un Français sur dix [The excluded: One in ten French].* Paris: Le Seuil.

Lugo-Gil, J., Yoshikawa, H., & Tamis-LeMonda, C. S. (2006). Assessing expenditures on children among low-income, immigrant and ethnically diverse families (Working Paper 06-36). Ann Arbor, MI: University of Michigan, National Poverty Center. Retrieved June 13, 2008, from http://npc.umich.edu/publications/u/working_paper06-36.pdf

McLoyd, V. C. (1990). The impact of economic hardship on Black families and children: Psychological distress, parenting, and socioemotional development. *Child Development, 61,* 311–346.

McLoyd, V. C. (1998). Socioeconomic disadvantage and child development. *American Psychologist, 5,* 185–204.

Micklewright, J. (2002). *Social exclusion and children: A European view for a U.S. debate.* Innocenti Centre Working Paper No. 90. Florence, Italy: UNICEF Innocenti Research Centre. Retrieved June 13, 2008, from *http://www.unicef-icdc.org/publications/pdf/iwp90.pdf*

Mistry, R., Vandewater, E., Huston, A. C., & McLoyd, V. C. (2002). Economic well-being and children's social adjustment: The role of family process in an ethnically diverse low-income sample. *Child Development, 73,* 935–951.

Mullen, E. (1995). *Mullen Scales of Early Learning.* Circle Pines, MN: American Guidance Society.

Nord, C. W., & Griffin, J. A. (1999). Educational profile of 3- to 8-year old children of immigrants. In D. Hernandez (Ed.), *Children of immigrants: Health, adjustment, and public assistance* (pp. 348–387). Washington, DC: National Academy Press.

Pessar, P. R., & Graham, P. M. (2002). Dominicans: Transnational identities and local politics. In N. Foner (Ed.), *New immigrants in New York* (pp. 251–273). New York: Russell Sage Foundation.

Preston, J. (2007, August 6). Immigration is at center of new laws around U.S. *The New York Times,* Section A, p. 12.

Raikes, H., Pan, B. A., Luze, G., Tamis-LeMonda, C. S., Brooks-Gunn, J., Constantine, J., et al. (2006). Mothers' bookreading in low-income familias: Correlates and outcomes during the first three years of life. *Child Development, 77,* 924–953.

Saraceno, C. (Ed.). (2002). *Social assistance dynamics in Europe: National and local welfare regimes.* Bristol, UK: Policy Press.

Schafer, J. L., & Graham, J. W. (2002). Missing data: Our view of the state of the art. *Psychological Methods, 7,* 147–177.

Sherraden, M. (1991). *Assets and the poor: A new American welfare policy.* Armonk, NY: M. E. Sharpe.

Shrout, P. E., & Bolger, N. (2002). Mediation in experimental and nonexperimental studies: New procedures and recommendations. *Psychological Methods, 7,* 422–445.

Smith, R. C. (2006). *Mexican New York: Transnational lives of new immigrants.* Berkeley, CA: University of California Press.

Suárez-Orozco, C. S., & Suarez-Orozco, M. M. (2001). *Children of immigration.* Cambridge, MA: Harvard University Press.

Suárez-Orozco, M. M. (1989). *Central American refugees and U.S. high schools: A psychosocial study of motivation and achievement.* Palo Alto, CA; Stanford University Press.

Way, N., Gingold, R., Rotenberg, M., & Kuriakose, G. (2005). Close friendships among urban, ethnic-minority adolescents. *New Directions in Child and Adolescent Development, 107,* 41–59.

Yeung, J., Linver, M. R., & Brooks-Gunn, J. (2002). How money matters for young children's development: Parental investment and family processes. *Child Development, 73,* 1861–1879.

Yoshikawa, H., Lugo-Gil, J., Chaudry, A., & Tamis-LeMonda, C. S. (2005, April). How lower-income immigrant families in New York City learn about and navigate U.S. programs and policies for families and children. Paper presented at the biennial meeting of the Society for Research in Child Development, Atlanta, GA.

Yoshikawa, H., McCartney, K., Myers, R., Bub, K., Lugo-Gil, J., Knaul, F., et al. (2008). Early childhood education in Mexico: Expansion, quality improvement, and curricular reform (UNICEF Innocenti Research Centre Working Paper 07/40). Florence, Italy: UNICEF Innocenti Research Centre. Retrieved June 13, 2008, from http://www.unicef-irc.org/publications/pdf/iwp_2007_03.pdf

Yoshikawa, H., & Rivera, A. C. (2007). Data on hardship and survival strategies among lower-income immigrant parents. Unpublished data, New York University, New York, NY.

HIROKAZU YOSHIKAWA is a professor of education at the Harvard Graduate School of Education.

ERIN B. GODFREY is a doctoral candidate in Community Psychology at New York University.

ANN C. RIVERA received her doctorate in Community Psychology from New York University and is currently a Society for Research in Child Development Public Policy Fellow.

NEW DIRECTIONS FOR CHILD AND ADOLESCENT DEVELOPMENT • DOI: 10.1002/cd

Suárez-Orozco, C., & Carhill, A. (2008). Afterword: New directions in research with immi-
grant families and their children. In H. Yoshikawa & N. Way (Eds.), Beyond the family:
Contexts of immigrant children's development. *New Directions for Child and Adolescent
Development, 121*, 87–104.

6

Afterword: New Directions in Research With Immigrant Families and Their Children

Carola Suárez-Orozco, Avary Carhill

Abstract

*Although migration is fundamentally a family affair, the family, as a unit of
analysis, has been understudied both by scholars of migration and by developmental psychologists. Researchers have often struggled to conceptualize immigrant children, adolescents, and their families, all too often giving way to
pathologizing them, ignoring generational and ethnic distinctions among immigrant groups, stereotyping immigrants as "problem" or (conversely) "model"
minorities, and overlooking the complexity of race, gender, documentation, and
language in their lives. In addition, contexts other than the family remain understudied. In this Afterword, the authors examine these issues, the contributions
of the chapters in this volume to understanding them, and their implications for
research and theory within the field of developmental science.* © 2008 Wiley
Periodicals, Inc.

M igration is fundamentally a family affair. More often than not, family obligations and family ties are the very foundation of the arduous immigrant voyage (Suárez-Orozco, Suárez-Orozco, & Todorova, 2008). The process of migration asserts tremendous stress upon the family members in a myriad of ways (Falicov, 1980, 1998; Suárez-Orozco & Suárez-Orozco, 2001; Suárez-Orozco et al., 2008). Yet the family, as a unit of analysis, has been understudied by scholars of migration (see García-Coll & Magnuson, 1997; Landale, 1997). In part, this may be linked to the challenge of conducting sound research with immigrant families given the magnitude, diversity, and complexity of the migratory phenomenon as well as the dearth of cross-culturally effective and meaningful research strategies (Hughes, Seidman, & Edwards, 1993).

For this reason, the current volume of *New Directions* represents an important achievement in the landscape of research on immigrant families and their children. After many years of neglect in the field of immigration research, developmentalists have come to recognize that 22% of our nation's children are immigrant children and that by 2040 projections indicate that one in three children will have an immigrant parent (Rong & Priessle, 1998). In many ways, the field of study on immigrant families and children is an emerging—one might even say exploding—field in developmental psychology today. The immigrant family and child, however, present a number of challenges for study. The current volume offers several examples of innovative attempts to address the unique challenges of understanding immigrants: the conceptualization of immigrants themselves, the role of social context, and the methodological means to accurately and insightfully do research with immigrants. Here we discuss the implications of these challenges for advancing theory and research about immigration, and we highlight ways in which the authors in this volume have engaged in scholarship that confronts these issues and concerns.

Emerging Directions in Research in the Field

Psychologists have arrived late on the scene. Family and person-centered aspects of migration—a logical purview of the discipline of psychology (and most particularly developmental psychology)—have only recently begun to systematically be examined within our discipline. At the eve of the 21st century, the scholarship of migration was dominated by demographers (focusing on where the new immigrants were from and where they were settling), economists (concerned with understanding the economic forces that push migrants from their homes and lure them to new destinations as well as establishing the fiscal and wage implications of immigrants for host society economies), sociologists (investigating how immigrants were adapting to the new society), and anthropologists (inquiring into what cultural practices the new immigrants brought with them and how those in the host society responded to them). With the exception of anthropologists and ethnographically savvy sociologists, these disciplinary gazes have for the most part taken a telescopic view.

The foci of the field of psychology have primarily been on the *adaptive process* as it is experienced either individually or within the family. Thus, pressing issues of concern in the field of psychology have until recently fallen into four broad domains: (a) acculturative stress and "migration morbidity," (b) relational strains in family dynamics, (c) challenges in identity formation, and (d) educational adaptations and outcomes.

Conceptualizing Immigrants

To paraphrase famed anthropologist Clyde Kluckhohn (1949), every immigrant is like all other immigrants, like some other immigrants, and like no other immigrant. The goal of research should be to capture the migratory experience in all of its subtleties—understanding that there are many common denominators of experience between the groups of origin while recognizing the specificity of experience of particular groups as well as individuals. Researchers have often struggled to conceptualize immigrants, all too often giving way to pathologizing immigrants, ignoring generational and ethnic distinctions among immigrant groups, stereotyping immigrants as "problem" and "model" minorities, and overlooking the complexity of race, gender, documentation, and language in the lives of immigrant families and youth. Following is an examination of these issues and their implications for research and theory within the field of psychology. We note the ways in which the authors in this volume have laudably moved beyond the overgeneralization or underdistinction that all too often occur in research in the field.

Pathology and Resilience. Psychologists in particular, but social scientists in general, often search for a link between the stresses of the migratory experience and an expected negative fall-out (depression, marital conflict, crises of identity, incarceration rates, and the like) resulting from that experience (Ainslie, 1998; Arrendondo-Dowd, 1980; Grinberg & Grinberg, 1990; Sluzki, 1979; Suárez-Orozco, 2000). (It should be noted that these outcomes would likely be more pronounced among refugees, but distinction between immigrants and refugees is rarely made within the field of psychology.) When sampling from a nonclinical population, however, the data that has emerged from this line of research has demonstrated thin evidence of a relationship between migration and psychopathology (Suárez-Orozco & Qin-Hilliard, 2004). Although few studies examine mental health issues in the country of origin, there is some evidence that there is not a significant difference between nonmigrants and migrants from that country in a new setting. Further, when comparing immigrants to nonimmigrants, it appears that on the whole immigrants do not demonstrate significantly higher rates of psychopathology than do nonimmigrants (Alegria, Sribney, Woo, Torres, & Guarnaccia, 2007; Breslau & Chang, 2006).

This general finding, that the link between migration and negative mental health outcomes is relatively weak, is consistent with growing evidence that the first generation, in fact, seem to do better on a variety of indicators of well-being when compared to the second, and to native-born peers (Davies & McKelvey, 1998: Hernández & Charney, 1998). Several large-scale international studies have replicated this epidemiological paradox in Canada (Beiser, Hou, Hyman, & Tousignant, 1999), New Zealand (Davies & McKelvey, 1998), and Europe. First-generation immigrants seem to do considerably better on a number of mental and physical health indicators despite higher poverty levels.

A number of potential explanations for this "immigrant paradox" have been advanced. There may be a selective pattern of migration—individuals with greater psychological and physical robustness may be more likely to embark on the immigrant journey. First-generation immigrants may also be engaging in healthier cultural practices than subsequent generations; across generations, immigrants may assimilate to less healthy habits—greater dependence on processed foods, employment that requires less physical exertion, greater likelihood of abusing substances, and the like.

Resilience may play a central role in these outcomes. Those in the first generation may be more likely to draw on the inoculating effects of the dual frame of reference between the country of origin and the new setting ("my lot is in substantive ways better here than there") (Suárez-Orozco & Suárez-Orozco, 1995) as well as hope (Suárez-Orozco & Suárez-Orozco, 2001). Further, the 1.5 generation and beyond may be made more vulnerable as a result of developing and growing up in the face of a negative social mirror and social disparagement that reflects back a distorted negative image of their worth and potential (Suárez-Orozco, 1998). Future studies that focus on the psychological sequelae of migration should consider both pathological outcomes as well as the particular strengths and resiliencies that emerge during the course of migration (Suárez-Orozco & Suárez-Orozco, 1995; Suárez-Orozco et al., 2008).

Generational Distinctions. The epidemiological paradox and other evidence underlines the importance of recognizing the differences between the first, the 1.5 generation, and the second generation and beyond in data collection and analyses. For example, second-generation Caribbean origin youth are significantly more susceptible to stereotype threat than are the first (Deaux, 2006). Rather than moving towards an Americanized identity, immigrant adolescents tend to maintain identities closely linked to their homeland with their countries of origin (Song, 2007). Much of the work on ethnic populations (Latinos and Asians) has simply ignored generational dimensions altogether.

Problem Versus Model Minorities. Research on immigrant origin groups tends to focus on problem populations. Research abounds around why Latinos (many of whom are of immigrant origin) are not doing better as a group in the educational system or how particular groups are overrepresented in prison or in gangs. Conversely, researchers also look towards the other end of the continuum—the model minority (Lee, 1996). Asian immigrants are often held up as the gold standard—why can't other groups do as well as the Asian students? This stereotype, while on the surface flattering, politically pits groups against one another and ignores the fact that many Asian-origin Americans struggle with structural barriers (Lee, 1996). To date, there has been little research on the psychological and social costs of being a model minority. In this volume (pp. 27–42), Qin, Way, and Rana poignantly reveal the social price that Chinese immigrants pay: while their teachers view them as "model minorities," their peers may resent them and subject them to relentless bullying.

Pan-Ethnic Confabulations. Much of the research that could shed light on the immigrant family experience examines pan-ethnic categories (such as Latinos, Asians, and Blacks). This kind of work, while important, loses sight of the wide variety of incoming resources and generational patterns that exist within these larger designations.

At over 43 million individuals, the Latino category encompasses well over half of all immigrants to the U.S. (U.S. Census Bureau, 2006). Latinos are extraordinarily diverse—some have ancestors who were established on what is now U.S. territory long before the current borders were set through conquest and land purchases. On the other hand, forty percent of Latinos are born abroad. Mexican Americans, Puerto Ricans, and Cubans have historically been the most represented groups in the aggregated Latino category. In recent decades, however, large numbers of Latinos have been immigrating from dozens of countries (such as Ecuador, Colombia, and Brazil) that fuel this burgeoning population. Today, an estimated two-thirds of Latinos are either immigrants or the children of immigrants (Suárez-Orozco & Paez, 2002). Many Latinos share Spanish as the common language of origin, but language loss is very rapid across generations; it is rare to encounter a completely fluent Spanish speaker by the third or even the second generation (Portes & Rumbaut, 2001). The sending countries, the areas of settlement, the historical timing of the migration, the political climate, and economic circumstances vary considerably for Latinos from different countries of origin. This array of backgrounds and experiences challenge any semblance of Latino homogeneity.

Asians are often represented as a monolith in research with no differentiation between the child of an Massachusetts Institute of Technology (MIT) professor from Taiwan or a Hmong refugee. The Asian population has grown rapidly since the 1990s in the United States, currently estimated to include 12.5 million people, totaling 4.3% of the U.S. population. This broad category includes individuals from China, the Philippines, Japan, Korea, Vietnam, Thailand, Laos, India, Pakistan, and Bangladesh, among other countries. These countries represent diverse cultural traditions, religious practices, and languages. While some are among the most educated (Indians on average have higher levels of educational attainment than do native-born U.S. citizens), while others have low levels of literacy (e.g., Laotians, Hmong, and individuals from the Fujian province of China). More than two thirds of Asians in the United States today are born abroad, yet some have been here for many generations and have high rates of intermarriage with native-born U.S. citizens (U.S. Census Bureau, 2006).

Blacks are unique in U.S. history; Africans were brought as involuntary migrants with the earliest Europeans. Currently, Blacks make up 12.8% of the total U.S. population. In 1900, only .02% of the Black population was of voluntary immigrant origin; today, this has changed considerably as African and West Indian/Caribbean immigrants account for over 6% of the Black population (Tormala & Deaux, 2006.) In New York, nearly half of the Black population is of immigrant origin from such diverse sending countries as Ghana, Jamaica, Guyana, and Haiti. Again, within this population there is tremendous diversity. On one end of the spectrum, a high proportion of Ghanaian doctors are practicing in New York rather than in their country where they were trained (Mullan, 2005), while many of the newest wave of Haitian immigrants have limited literacy and interrupted schooling. Some arrive with elite experiences while others have encountered tremendous violence and arrive suffering from posttraumatic stress. These sending experiences have implications for family life and adaptation to the new society.

Gendered Patterns of Adaptation. Gendered migratory experiences are another domain of significant neglect within the immigration research community (Donato, Gabaccia, Holdaway, Manalansan, & Pessar, 2006). Scholars all too often fail to consider whether women are motivated by the same forces as men, and how their experience within the new context may or may not be different from that of their male counterparts. There is ample evidence to suggest that there are many dimensions of experience, which are indeed different for men and women (Hongdagneu-Sotelo, 1999; Mahler, 1999; Pessar, 1989). Girls and young women demonstrate more favorable academic trajectories than do young men (Suárez-Orozco et al., 2008), who often must contend with more unforgiving, hostile reception within the new country (López, 2002; Suárez-Orozco & Qin, 2006).

On the other hand, assuming that gender will always lead to different experiences is a mistake. While there certainly are differences between immigrant males and females there also are many similarities (Cornell, 2000; Suárez-Orozco & Qin-Hilliard, 2004; Suárez-Orozco & Qin, 2006). Interestingly, many of the dimensions we have examined over the years have revealed no gender differences. Hence, although it is important to consider gender, it is also important to recognize that non-findings of overlap in attitudes, behaviors, and experiences are in some ways as interesting as findings of differences. Future research should consider how, when, and why it makes a difference to be an immigrant or to be from a particular country or to be female rather than male (Eckes & Trautner, 2000; Suárez-Orozco & Qin-Hilliard, 2004; Suárez-Orozco & Qin, 2006).

Racialized Experiences. Overlooking the racialized experiences of immigrants is another serious oversight in much research. Immigrants encounter very different receptions depending upon whether or not they are "racially marked" by phenotype (Bailey, 2001; López, 2002; Waters, 1999).

Given the color spectrum represented by the new immigrants, keeping this perspective in mind is essential while conducting research into the adaptation of new immigrants in a racially conscious society.

Documentation Among Immigrant Origin Youth. For immigrants of the first generation, undocumented status can be a very real hardship. Currently, there are an estimated 12 million undocumented in the United States. Approximately half of foreign-born Mexican children are estimated to be undocumented. Students often arrive in the United States after multiple family separations and traumatic border-crossings. Once settled, they may continue to experience fear and anxiety about being apprehended, being deported, and again being separated from their parents. Such emotional duress takes its toll on undocumented youth. Undocumented students with dreams of graduating from high school and going on to college will find that their legal status stands in the way of their access to postsecondary education. Waters are muddied by the fact that within the same family, the parents and siblings may be undocumented while some siblings are documented. Although this is a topic of tremendous import, it is a challenge to conduct research in this area as it is difficult to ask participants to report their status. Kalil and Chen (pp. 43–62) and Yoshikawa and his colleagues (pp. 73–96) are to be commended for taking on this tremendously important topic.

Seasonal Migration. Data suggest that approximately 600,000 children travel with their migrant parents in the United States each year. Youth in seasonal migrant families face particular challenges. They experience multiple moves, frequent interruptions in schooling, as well as particularly harsh working and living conditions. Migrant children are the least likely to be enrolled in school. The lack of continuity in schooling (because of interruptions during the school year, the difficulty of transferring school records, health problems, and lack of English language skills) contributes to their low attendance and to the particularly high dropout rate among seasonal migrant children. The dropout rate after sixth grade among these children is twice the national average and typically they only reach the eighth grade. This is a topic that is difficult to tackle due to the transience of the population, but clearly has serious policy implications.

Linguistic Barriers and Opportunities. Most immigrant youth are second language learners. The complex task of learning the kinds of English used in school takes longer than most realize. In a comparative sample of first-generation immigrant youth who had been in school in the United States for 7 years on average, only 7% had developed academic English skills comparable to those of their native-born English-speaking peers (Carhill, Suárez-Orozco, & Paez, in press; Suárez-Orozco et al., 2008). English language difficulties present particular challenges for optimal performance in the current context of high stakes tests. Performance on tests such as the Texas Assessment of Academic Skills (TAAS) in Texas, the Regents exam in New York, and the Massachusetts Comprehensive Assessment System (MCAS) in Massachusetts have implications for college access. Scholastic

Aptitude Tests (SATs) are also a challenge and serve to limit access to the more competitive colleges. Second language acquisition issues can mask the actual skills and knowledge of immigrant youth in both oral and written displays. Even when immigrant students are able to participate in mainstream classrooms and postsecondary education, their academic English language skills may still be developing, and they may struggle, missing subtleties in lectures and discussions, reading more slowly than native speakers, and having trouble in academic writing. This is likely to bring down their grades, in turn, impacting access to further educational opportunities.

Contextual Challenges. Little work has examined larger constructions of social context. By and large, the context of origin (Rumbaut, 1997)—including the economic, political, cultural, social, and personal factors that may have propelled the immigrants to leave their country of origin—are often ignored by psychologists. The contexts of reception (Rumbaut, 1997)—national integration policies; legal frameworks; the political climate; the media representations about immigrants—also has not seemed to be of particular focus of interest (cf. Deaux, 2006). But context matters.

In the following sections poverty, neighborhoods, schools, and relational contexts will be examined specifically as they relate to immigrant youth and families. Additionally, the issues of documentation and language will be considered. This volume serves to deepen the conversation beyond the usual family and school contexts for immigrant families and their children. Specifically, chapters within this volume address such topics as "What levels of access to institutional resources are reported by low-income Dominican and Mexican parents?" "How do Chinese American families utilize family resources to support their children's success at school?" "What factors predict mothers' plans for their children's transnational travel?"

Poverty. Poverty is a reality for large numbers of immigrant youth. Nearly a quarter of the children of immigrants live below the poverty line—in comparison to 11 percent for non-Hispanic whites. Nationwide, 37 percent of the children of immigrants report difficulties affording food and are more than 4 times as likely than native-born children to live in crowded housing conditions. They are twice as likely as native-born children to be uninsured and 3 times less likely to have a source of regular health care (Capps, 2001). Those living in poverty often experience major life event stress as well as the stress of daily hassles. Poverty frequently coexists with a variety of other factors that augment risks—such as single-parenthood, residence in neighborhoods plagued with violence, gang activity, and drug trade as well as school environments that are segregated, overcrowded, and poorly funded. The effects of immigrant poverty have long been recognized as a significant risk factor for youth development (Luthar, 1999). Children raised in circumstances of socioeconomic deprivation are vulnerable to an array of psychological distresses, including difficulties concentrating and sleeping, anxiety, and depression, as well as a heightened propensity for delinquency and violence.

Poverty might be a preexisting condition prior to migration, or it may be temporarily accentuated as immigrants experience some downward mobility in the process of settlement. In an effort to untangle these issues, Kalil and Chen (pp. 43–62) ask to what extent food insecurity is related to immigrant status among low-income households.

Neighborhood Contexts. Where immigrants settle will have profound implications for the experiences and adaptation of immigrant youth. Immigrants—especially Latino and Caribbean new arrivals—are settling in large numbers in highly segregated, deep-poverty, urban settings (Orfield & Yun, 1999). The degree of segregation and experienced discrimination will have a series of consequences (Massey & Denton, 1993). New immigrants of color who settle in predominantly minority neighborhoods will have virtually no direct, systematic, and intimate contact with middle-class white Americans. This in turn will affect the kinds of English encountered by the youth, the quality of schools they will attend, and the networks that are useful to access desirable colleges and jobs (Orfield, 1995; Portes & Hao, 1996).

Concentrated poverty is associated with the "disappearance of meaningful work opportunities" (Wilson, 1997). Youngsters in such neighborhoods are chronically underemployed or unemployed and must search for work elsewhere. In neighborhoods with few opportunities in the formal economy, underground or informal activities tend to flourish. Exposure to violence in both neighborhoods and schools is an everyday reality for many immigrant youth today (Collier, 1998). Sociologists Alejandro Portes and Rubén Rumbaut have argued that these structural features interact and conspire to generate a pattern they have termed "segmented assimilation," whereby, over time, large numbers of poor immigrant youth of color will tend to assimilate toward the American underclass rather than assimilating to middle-class norms (Portes & Rumbaut, 2001). As Yoshikawa, Godfrey, and Rivera (pp. 63–86) suggest, access to institutional resources is entangled with such structural factors and has serious implications for immigrant youth from a young age and on.

School Contexts. Neighborhood characteristics are directly reflected in the schools attended by immigrant children and youth. Immigrant youth today enroll in schools that cover the range from well functioning, with a culture of high expectations and a focus on achievement, to dysfunctional institutions characterized by ever-present fear of violence, distrust, low expectations, and institutional anomie. Unfortunately, poor immigrant youth who need the most academic help tend to enroll in inferior schools with triple segregation—by poverty, race, and language (Orfield & Lee, 2006). These poorly resourced schools offer the least opportunities to the students who most need them (Orfield & Lee, 2006; Suárez-Orozco et al., 2008).

Students' experiences in schools have academic as well as health consequences (Currie, Hurrelmann, Settertobulte, Smith, & Todd, 2000; Samdal, Nutbeam, Wold, & Kannas, 1998). A stressful school climate, characterized by perceptions of academic pressure, danger, discrimination, and the absence of supportive relationships, can directly affect students' well-being, who might begin to feel that the requirements of the environment tax their abilities to cope (Karatzias, Power, Flemming, & Lennan, 2002). Stress in the school environment is an important contributor to health problems and psychosomatic symptoms in students and exerts its effects through a combination of individual and contextual-level factors (Torsheim & Wold, 2001).

On the other hand, the educational context can be a source of self-esteem (Karatzias et al., 2002) and social support, which can have a protective effect on students' well-being (Samdal et al., 1998). Current research is directed toward identifying school characteristics and educational experiences that can have detrimental or enhancing effects on well-being (Currie et al., 2000; Karatzias et al., 2002). The educational context can be perceived differently for students from different cultural backgrounds, and thus the consequences need to be studied with a sensitivity to cross-cultural differences in values and expectations for education (Collier, 1998).

Relational Contexts.   From the time of arrival in their new country, networks of relationships provide families with tangible aid (such as baby sitting or making a loan), as well as guidance and advice (including information, job, and housing leads). These supports are particularly critical for newcomers for whom many aspects of the new environment can initially be quite disorienting. Relationships also serve a critical function in maintaining and enhancing self-esteem, while providing acceptance, approval, and a sense of belonging. For children and youth, relationships play a particularly important role in sustaining motivation and engagement in school (Suárez-Orozco & Suárez-Orozco, 1995; Suárez-Orozco et al., 2008). In turn, academic engagement and achievement can strengthen the supportive relationships from which they stem—immigrant students are typically motivated to achieve for their families whom they often understand as having sacrificed so that they themselves may have better opportunities (Suárez-Orozco & Suárez-Orozco, 1995; Suárez-Orozco et al., 2008).

The deeply textured work of Li, Holloway, Bempechat, and Loh in this volume (pp. 9–25) demonstrates how the family is a significant gravitational field in the lives of youth. Family cohesion and the maintenance of a well-functioning system of supervision, authority, and mutuality is a powerful vector in shaping the well-being and social outcomes of children. Although parents play the central role in traditional two-parent nuclear mainstream American family systems, immigrant families often involve a larger cast of characters. For many immigrant families, extended family members— godparents, aunts, uncles, older cousins, and the like—are often critical sources of tangible instrumental and emotional support. Immigrant families are complex in structure, challenging the usual definitions of family in social science (intact, mother-headed, blended, and the like). Many, if not most immigrant families include multiple generations, and there tends to be much fluidity in membership from one point of time to the next. Thus, a cross-sectional study would capture a very different picture of the same family than would a longitudinal study that asked the same question about

NEW DIRECTIONS FOR CHILD AND ADOLESCENT DEVELOPMENT • DOI: 10.1002/cd

family composition annually. There is also tremendous variation by country of origin and by social class. Thus, simply defining the family unit is a methodological challenge in itself.

What specifically constitutes family involvement is another critical question that was elegantly addressed in the Li et al. chapter. Due to linguistic challenges and work schedule restrictions many immigrant parents may not be able to help their children complete their homework as middle-class mainstream native-born parents often do. Chinese families, building on cultural models that they bring with them, have been able to harness resources outside the family to help their children succeed, deftly demonstrated by Li and colleagues.

Because no family is an island, family cohesion and functioning are enhanced when the family is part of a larger community displaying effective forms of what Felton Earls has termed "community agency" (Earls, 1997). In immigrant communities these organizations are often associated with a church or religious organization (often overlooked by social scientists). For youth, the notion of community cohesion and supervision are conceptualized as inoculating to toxic elements in their new settings (DeVos, 1992). Zhou and Li, in an earlier volume of New Directions, argued that community organizations serving Latino immigrant origin youth tend to be reactive, emphasizing problem behaviors such as gang or pregnancy prevention; in contrast, community services for Asian youth are proactive, emphasizing activities such as SAT preparation, math, and English tutoring (Zhou & Li, 2003). Li et al. (pp. 9–25) describe the unique ways in which family and community forces are conjoined positively and proactively.

Mentoring relationships often evolve organically in a variety of contexts and make a tremendous difference in adolescents' lives (Rhodes, 2002; Suárez-Orozco et al., 2008). In stressed families with limited social resources, mentors can serve to support healthier family and peer relationships by alleviating pressure on the family (Roffman, Suárez-Orozco, & Rhodes, 2003). Mentoring relationships could particularly be useful in serving newly arrived immigrant youth. A bicultural mentor can serve as a bridge between the old and new cultures. An acculturated mentor can act as fount of information about the new cultural rules of engagement. Mentoring relationships can serve to heal ruptures in relationships that have resulted from long separations and complicated reunifications. Because immigrant adolescents' parents may not be available given their work schedules, the guidance and affection from a mentor can serve to fill the void. Mentoring relationships have been shown to reduce substance abuse, aggressive behavior, and incidences of delinquency (Rhodes, 2002). College educated mentors can help their protégés to perform better in school by helping them with homework and by providing informed advice about college access. Indeed, we have found that among newcomer immigrant students who were successful, in almost every case behind the scenes there were informal mentors, successful relatives, and community leaders who served to guide the way (Suárez-Orozco et al., 2008).

Peers can serve as both positive and negative social capital (Portes & Hao, 1998). On the positive side of the equation, they can provide an emotional sense of belonging and acceptance, and provide tangible help with homework assignments, language translations, and orientation to school (Gibson, Gándara, & Koyama, 2004; Stanton-Salazar, 2004). To newly arrived immigrant students, the companionship of co-national friends seemed to be especially important, as these peers served as important sources of information on school culture (Suárez-Orozco, Pimentel, Martin, in press). Hence, peers can act as "vital conduits" (Stanton-Salazar, 2004) of information to disoriented newcomer students. Peers also can serve as buffers to loneliness and embarrassment and as bolsterers of self-confidence and self-efficacy providing emotional sustenance that supported the development of significant psychosocial competencies (Suárez-Orozco et al., 2008).

On the other hand, while some peers model positive academic behavior and establish constructive academic norms, others serve to distract their classmates from performing optimally in school (Gibson et al., 2004). Peers may encourage maladaptive academic behavior, promote drug use, and discourage competent academic behavior. Peers may contribute to unsafe school and community environments, which can undermine students' ability to concentrate, their sense of security, and their ability to experience trusting relationships in school. Further, as Qin, Way, and Rana demonstrate in this volume (pp. 27–42), co-ethnic peers may not always come together to establish a dense and supportive network, even in the face of sustained harassment.

Methodological Challenges

Cross-cultural research on immigrants forces us to reexamine many of the traditional social science assumptions around validity and reliability (McLoyd & Steinberg, 1998; Suárez-Orozco & Suárez-Orozco, 1995). There is a growing consensus in the field of cross-cultural research that mixed method designs, linking emic (outsider) and etic (insider) approaches, triangulating data, and embedding emerging findings into an ecological framework, are essential to this endeavor (Bronfenbrenner 1988; Hughes, Seidman, & Edwards, 1993; Doucette-Gates, Brooks-Gunn, & Chase-Lansdale, 1998; Branch, 1999; Suárez-Orozco et al., 2008; Sue & Sue, 1987).

Interdisciplinary Collaborations. Migrations are complex and outcomes are multiply determined. We must recognize that this domain requires interdisciplinary, mixed-method strategies to achieve any depth. We have much to learn from our colleagues in allied fields of economics, sociology, anthropology, public health, and linguistics. Interdisciplinary teams whose members are bilingual (or multilingual) lead to more robust research contributions. Team members must be well versed in one another's methodologies. Just as is the case with language abilities, it is rare that complete mastery (with equal ease in reading, writing, and oral fluency) is achieved in both languages. Thus, it is important to have multidisciplinary teams where there is at least one member who is dominant in one language/discipline, but who is also quite fluent (with a high level of understanding) in the other language(s).

The contributors to this volume take decisive strides in the direction our field must take as it tackles the important and complex issues immigrant families and youth encounter. The researchers here make a concerted effort to take on multidisciplinary perspectives and to work across disciplines.

Etic & Emic Perspectives. Combining "outsider" (etic) and "insider" (emic) approaches to diverse populations is important in the phases of both data collection and analysis (Cooper, Jackson, Azmitia, & Lopez, 1998). Bicultural and bilingual researchers are better able to establish rapport and trust within the communities and gain entry into immigrant populations that might otherwise be difficult to access. Further, insiders are essential for appropriate linguistic and cultural translations of protocols. Their perspective is also essential to accurate and culturally relevant interpretations. If the research is not conducted by members of the immigrant community, it is essential that cultural experts be consulted in both the development of instruments as well as the interpretation of findings. Outsiders provide a fresh interpretive perspective and may lend specific disciplinary expertise. Interpretive communities of "insiders" and "outsiders" as well as individuals representing a range of disciplinary expertise are highly recommended. Li et al. (pp. 9–25) provide a noteworthy example of a collaborative effort between community insiders and outsiders.

Culturally Sensitive Tools. Questions and prompts that are valid for one group may not be valid for another. It is a challenge to develop single instruments or approaches that capture the experiences of individuals from a variety of backgrounds. Of course, research protocols should always be provided in the language of dominance of the informant. Measures developed with mainstream English-speaking populations (as are many standardized instruments) are often culturally and linguistically biased (Doucette-Gates, Brooks-Gunn, & Chase-Lansdale, 1998). New tools, either adapted from preexisting instruments or developed entirely anew, are often a necessity for accurate research with immigrants. The process of development should be dynamic and inductive, involving theoretically based formulations along with themes emerging from the field. As culturally informed questionnaires are developed they must be careful translated and piloted.

Triangulated Data. Using triangulated data, from a variety of perspectives, using a variety of strategies is crucial when faced with the challenges of validity in conducting research with groups of diverse backgrounds. Such an approach allows more confidence that data is accurately capturing the phenomenon under consideration. By sifting through a variety of perspectives—self reports, parent reports, teacher reports (in the case of youth), or other community members (in the case of adults) as well as researcher observations—concurrence and disconnections can be established between what informants say they do, what others say they do, and what the researcher sees them do. Researchers should consider various levels of analysis in their research including the individual, interpersonal relations (peers, family), context-specific social groups (work, schools, neighborhood, church), as well as cultural dimensions.

Longitudinal Perspectives. Cross-sectional data limits our ability to detect changes over time. Though time consuming and expensive, longitudinal research has much to offer and should be pursued when possible (Fuligni, 2001; Suárez-Orozco, 2001; Suárez-Orozco et al., 2008). The study by Yoshikawa, Godfrey, and Rivera (pp. 63–86) is drawn from a longitudinal data set, which will allow for an accumulation of rich analysis over time. Through their ongoing work with the Early Childhood Cohort Study in New York, findings such as the transnational travel of immigrant families may be deepened into portraits of the impact of those early journeys on social networks, access to institutional resources, and success in school.

Comparison Samples. Whenever possible it is important to include comparison groups (Suárez-Orozco & Suárez-Orozco, 1995). These comparison groups can include both a range of immigrant origin populations as well as others from nonimmigrant populations who encounter similar contexts. These comparison groups provide valuable contextualization of findings. Throughout this volume, there are examples of research across groups: Gaytan, Xue, and Yoshikawa compared Dominican, Mexican, and Chinese mothers to determine patterns in mother's transnational migration plans. The return journey of Chinese babies emerged as a key finding. Kalil and Chen (pp. 43–62) modeled the relationship between food insecurity and mother's citizenship status through a careful comparison of various immigrant family configurations and across ethnic groups. Comparing access to various resources and outcomes among Dominican, Mexican, and African American families, Yoshikawa, Godfrey, and Rivera (pp. 63–86) found that although Mexican families had the least access to institutional resources, they reported the least economic hardship across groups.

Here we have outlined what historically have been some of the gaps in research on immigrant families and children and have made a number of recommendations for future research. Meaningful understanding requires insights provided by parallel fields within the social sciences. Interdisciplinary, triangulated research is essential to begin to unpack the nuanced effects of migration on families and youth, considering its particular challenges as well as its protective characteristics.

Using multidisciplinary strategies the authors in this volume address social contexts outside the usual suspects of family and school (e.g., peers, adult social networks, legal contexts). They examine a range of outcomes that are both :onventional (e.g., cognitive development and learning) as well as quite novel (e.g., food insecurity and infant travel). This volume makes a most valuable contribution to our understanding of contextual factors lying outside the family, shedding light on variations in developmental competencies among immigrant youth.

References

Ainslie, R. (1998). Cultural mourning, immigration, and engagement: vignettes from the Mexican experience. In M. M. Suárez-Orozco (Ed.), *Crossings: Mexican immigration in interdisciplinary perspectives* (pp. 283–300). Cambridge, MA: Harvard University Press, David Rockefeller Center for Latin American Studies.

Alegria, M., Sribney, W., Woo, M., Torres, M., & Guarnaccia, P. (2007). Looking beyond nativity: The relation of age of immigration, length of residence, and birth cohorts to the risk of onset of psychiatric disorders for Latinos. *Research in Human Development, 4*(1–2), 19–47.

Arredondo-Dowd, P. (1980). *The development process in the bilingual immigrant adolescent's identity search*. Unpublished manuscript.

Bailey, B. H. (2001). Dominican-American ethnic/racial identities and United States social categories. *International Migration Review, 35,* 677–708.

Beiser, M., Dion, R., Gotowiec, A., Hyman, I., & Vu, N. (1995, March). Immigrant and refugee children in Canada. *Canadian Journal of Psychiatry, 40,* 67–72.

Branch, C. W. (1999). Race and human development. *Racial and ethnic identity in school practices: Aspects of human development* (pp. 7–28). Mahwah, NJ: Erlbaum.

Breslau, J., & Chang, D. F. (2006). Psychiatric disorders among foreign-born and US-born Asian-Americans in a US national survey. *Social Psychiatry and Psychiatric Epidemiology, 41*(12), 943–950.

Bronfenbrenner, U. (1988). Forward. In R. Pence (Ed.), *Ecological research with children and families: Concepts to methodology* (pp. ix–xix). New York: Teachers College Press.

Capps, R. (2001). *Hardship among children of immigrants: Findings from the 1999 National Survey of America's Families*. Washington, DC: The Urban Institute.

Carhill, A., Súarez-Orozco, C., & Paez, M. (in press). Explaining English language proficiency among newcomer immigrant adolescents. *American Educational Research Journal*.

Collier, M. (1998). *Cultures of violence in Miami-Dade public schools*. Miami, FL: Florida International University.

Cooper, C. R., Jackson, J. F., Azmitia, M., & Lopez, E. M. (1998). Multiple selves, multiple worlds: Three useful strategies for research with ethnic minority youth on identity, relationship and opportunity structures. In V. McCloyd & L. Steinberg (Eds.), *Studying minority adolescents: Conceptual, methodological, and theoretical issues* (pp. 111–125). Mahwah, NJ: Erlbaum.

Cornell, R. W. (2000). *Men and boys*. Berkeley, CA: University of California Press.

Currie, C., Hurrelmann, K., Settertobulte, W., Smith, R., & Todd, J. (2000). *Health and health behaviour among young people*. WHO Policy Series: Health policy for children and adolescents. Copenhagen: WHO Regional Office.

Davies, L. C., & McKelvey, R. S. (1998). Emotional and behavioral problems and competencies among immigrant and non-immigrant adolescents. *Australian and New Zealand Journal of Psychiatry, 32,* 658–665.

Deaux, K. (2006). *To be an immigrant*. New York: Russell Sage Foundation.

DeVos, G., & Suárez-Orozco, M. (1992). *Social cohesion and alienation: Minorities in the United States and Japan*. Boulder, CO: Westview Press.

Donato, K., Gabaccia, D., Holdaway, J., Manalansan, M., & Pessar, P. (2006). Glass half full? Gender in migration studies [Special issue]. *International Migration Review, 40,* 3–26.

Doucette-Gates, A., Brooks-Gunn, J., & Chase-Lansdale, L. P. (1998). The role of bias and equivalence in the study of race, class, and ethnicity (pp. 211–236). In V. C.

McLoyd & L. Steinberg (Eds.), *Studying minority adolescents: Conceptual, methodological, and theoretical issues*. Mahwah, NJ: Erlbaum.

Earls, F. (1997, November/December). Tighter, safer, neighborhoods. *Harvard Magazine*, pp. 14–15.

Eckes, T., & Trautner, H. M. (Eds.). (2000). *The developmental social psychology of gender*. Mahwah, NJ: Erlbaum.

Falicov, C. J. (1980). Cultural variations in the family life cycle: The Mexican American family. In M. McGoldrick (Ed.), *The family life cycle: A framework for family therapy*. New York: Gardner Press.

Falicov, C. J. (1998). *Latino families in therapy: A guide to multicultural practices*. New York: Guilford Press.

Fuligni, A. (2001). A comparative longitudinal approach to acculturation among children from immigrant families. *Harvard Educational Review, 71*(3), 566–578.

García-Coll, C., & Magnuson, K. (1997). The psychological experience of immigration: A developmental perspective. In A. Booth, A. C. Crouter, & N. Landale (Eds.), *Immigration and the family: Research and policy on U.S. immigrants* (pp. 91–131). Mahwah, NJ: Erlbaum.

Gibson, M., Gandara, P., & Koyama, J. P. (2004). *School connections: U.S. Mexican youth, peers, and school adjustment*. New York: Teacher's College Press.

Grinberg, L., & Grinberg, R. (1990). *Psychoanalytic perspectives on migration and exile*. New Haven, CT: Yale University Press.

Hernández, D., & Charney, E. (Eds.). (1998). *From generation to generation: The health and well-being of children of immigrant families*. Washington, DC: National Academy Press.

Hongdagneu-Sotelo, P. (1999). Gender and contemporary U.S. immigration. *American Behavioral Scientist, 42*, 565–576.

Hughes, D., Seidman, E., & Edwards, D. (1993). Cultural phenomena and the research enterprise: Toward a culturally anchored methodology. *American Journal of Community Psychology, 21*, 687–703.

Karatzias, A., Power, K. G., Flemming, J., & Lennan, F. (2002). The role of demographics, personality variables and school stress on predicting school satisfaction/dissatisfaction: Review of the literature and research findings. *Educational Psychology, 22*(1), 33–50.

Kluckhohn, C. (1949). *Mirror for man: The relation of anthropology to modern life*. New York: Whitssley House.

Landale, N. S. (1997). Immigration and the family: An overview. In A. Booth, Ann C. Crouter, & Nancy Landale (Ed.), *Immigration and the family* (pp. 281–292). Mahwah, NJ: Erlbaum.

Lee, S. (1996). *Unraveling the "model minority" stereotype: Listening to Asian American youth*. New York: Teachers College Press.

López, N. (2002). *Hopeful girls, troubled boys: Race and gender disparity in urban education*. New York: Routledge.

Luthar, S. (1999). *Poverty and children's adjustment*. Thousand Oaks, CA: Sage.

Mahler, S. J. (1999). Engendering transnational migration: A case study of Salvadorans. *American Behavioral Scientist, 42*(4), 690–719.

Massey, D. S., & Denton, N. A. (1993). *American apartheid: Segregation and the making of the underclass*. Harvard University Press, Cambridge, MA.

McLoyd, V., & Steinberg, L. (Eds.). (1998). *Studying minority adolescents: Conceptual, methodological, and theoretical issues*. Mahwah, NJ: Erlbaum.

Mullan, F. (2005). The metrics of the physician brain drain. *The New England Journal of Medicine, 353*, 1810–1818.

Orfield, G. (1995). *Latinos in education: Recent trends*. Unpublished manuscript, Harvard Graduate School of Education, Cambridge, MA.

Orfield, G., & Lee, C. (2006). *Racial transformation and the changing nature of segregation*. Cambridge, MA: The Civil Rights Project at Harvard University.

Orfield, G., & Yun, J. T. (1999). *Resegregation in American schools.* Cambridge, MA: The Civil Rights Project at Harvard University.

Pessar, P. (1989). The Dominicans: Women in the household and the garment industry. In N. Foner (Ed.), *New immigrants in New York* (pp. 103–130). Santa Fe, NM: School for American Research.

Portes, A. (2000). The two meanings of social capital. *Sociological Forum, 15*(1), 1–12.

Portes, A., & Hao, L. (1998). E pluribus unum: Bilingualism and loss in the second generation. *Sociology of Education, 71*(11), 269–294.

Portes, A., & Rumbaut, R. G. (2001). *Legacies: The story of the second generation.* Berkeley: University of California Press.

Rhodes, J. E. (2002). *Stand by me: The risks and rewards of youth mentoring relationships.* Cambridge, MA: Harvard University Press.

Roffman, J., Suárez-Orozco, C., & Rhodes, J. (2003). Facilitating positive development in immigrant youth: The role of mentors and community organizations. In D. Perkins, L. M. Borden, J. G. Keith, & F. A. Villaruel (Eds.), *Positive youth development: Creating a positive tomorrow.* Brockton, MA: Kluwer Press.

Rong, X. L., & Preissle, J. (1998). *Educating immigrant students: What we need to know to meet the challenges.* Thousand Oaks, CA: Corwin Press.

Rumbaut, R. G. (1997). Ties that bind: Immigration and immigrant families in the United States. In A. Booth, Ann C. Crouter, & Nancy Landale (Eds.), *Immigration and the family* (pp. 3–46). Mahwah, NJ: Erlbaum.

Samdal, O., Nutbeam, D., Wold, B., & Kannas, L. (1998). Achieving health and educational goals through schools—a study of the importance of school climate and the student's satisfaction with school. *Health Education Research, 13*(3), 383–397.

Sluzki, C. (1979). Migration and family conflict. *Family Process, 18,* 379–390.

Song, S. (2007). Finding one's place: *Shifting ethnic identities of immigrant children from China, Haiti, and Mexico.* Unpublished doctoral disseration, Harvard Graduate School of Education, Cambridge, MA.

Stanton-Salazar, R. D. (2001). *Manufacturing hope and despair: The school and kin support networks of U.S.-Mexican youth.* New York/London: Teachers College Press.

Stanton-Salazar, R. D. (2004). Social capital among working-class minority students. In M. A. Gibson, P. Gándara, & J. P. Koyma (Eds.), *School connections: U.S. Mexican Youth, Peer, & School Achievement.* New York: Teacher's College Press.

Suárez-Orozco, C. (1998, Winter). The transitions of immigration: How are they different for women and men? Cambridge, MA: *Harvard University, David Rockefeller Center for Latin American Studies.*

Suárez-Orozco, C. (2000). Identities under siege: Immigration stress and social mirroring among the children of immigrants. In A. Robben & M. Suárez-Orozco (Eds.), *Cultures under siege: Social violence & trauma* (pp. 194–226). Cambridge, MA: Cambridge University Press.

Suárez-Orozco, C. (2001). Afterward: Understanding and serving the children of immigrants. *Harvard Educational Review, 71*(3), 579–589.

Suárez-Orozco, C., Pimentel, A., & Martin, M. (in press). The significance of relationships: Academic engagement and achievement among newcomer immigrant youth. In J. Holdoway & R. Alba (Eds.), *Special Issue,* Teachers College Press.

Suárez-Orozco, C., & Qin, D. B. (2006). Psychological & gendered perspectives on immigrant origin youth [Special issue]. *International Migration Review, 40,* 165–199.

Suárez-Orozco, C., & Qin-Hilliard, D. B. (2004). The cultural psychology of academic engagement: Immigrant boys' experiences in U.S. schools. In N. Way & J. Chu (Eds.), *Adolescent boys: Exploring diverse cultures of boyhood.* New York: New York University Press.

Suárez-Orozco, C., & Suárez-Orozco, M. (1995). *Transformations: Immigration, family life, and achievement motivation among Latino adolescents.* Stanford CA: Stanford University Press.

Suárez-Orozco, C., & Suárez-Orozco, M. (2001). *Children of immigration* (4th ed.). Cambridge, MA: Harvard University Press.

Suárez-Orozco, C., Suárez-Orozco, M., & Todorova, I. (2008). *Learning a new land: Immigrant students in American society.* Cambridge, MA: Harvard University Press.

Suárez-Orozco, M., & Paez, M. (2002). *Latinos: Remaking America.* Berkeley: University of California Press.

Sue, D., & Sue, S. (1987). Cultural factors in the clinical assessment of Asian Americans. *Journal of Consulting and Clinical Psychology, 55,* 479–487.

Tormala, T. T., & Deaux, K. (2006). Black immigrants to the United States: Confronting and constructing ethnicity and race. In R. Mahalingam (Ed.), *Cultural psychology of immigrants* (pp. 131–150). Mahwah, NJ: Erlbaum.

Torsheim, T., & Wold, B. (2001). School-related stress, support, and objective health complaints among early adolescents: A multilevel approach. *Journal of Adolescence, 24*(6), 701–713.

U.S. Census Bureau. (2006). *The 2005 American Community Survey.* Washington, DC: Author.

Waters, M. (1999). *Black identities: West Indian dreams and American realities.* Cambridge, MA: Harvard University Press.

Wilson, W. (1997). *When work disappears: The world of the new urban poor.* New York: Vintage Books.

Zhou, M., & Li, X. Y. (2003). Ethnic language schools and the development of supplementary education in the immigrant Chinese community in the United States. In C. Suárez-Orozco & I. Todorova (Eds.), *Understanding the Social Worlds of Immigrant Youth: New Directions for Youth Development* (Vol. 100). New York: Jossey-Bass.

CAROLA SUÁREZ-OROZCO *is a professor of applied psychology and Co-Director of Immigration Studies at New York University, New York.*

AVARY CARHILL *is a doctoral candidate in Applied Linguistics at the New York University Steinhardt School of Culture, Education, and Human Development, New York, NY.*

INDEX

For a complete list of back issues, please visit www.josseybass..com/go/ndcad

CAD 120 **The Intersections of Personal and Social Identities**
Margarita Azmitia, Moin Syed, Kimberley Radmacher, Editors
This volume brings together an interdisciplinary set of social scientists who are pioneering ways to research and theorize the connections between personal and social identity development in children, adolescents, and emerging adults. The authors of the seven chapters address the volume's three goals: (1) illustrating how theory and research in identity develop-ment are enriched by an interdisciplinary approach, (2) providing a rich developmental picture of personal and social identity development, and (3) examining the connections among multiple identities. Several chapters provide practical suggestions for individuals, agencies, and schools and universities that work with children, adolescents, and emerging adults in diverse communities across the United States.
ISBN 978-04703-72838

CAD 119 **Social Class and Transitions to Adulthood**
Jeylan T. Mortimer, Editor
This volume of *New Directions for Child and Adolescent Development* is inspired by a stirring address that Frank Furstenberg delivered at the 2006 Meeting of the Society for Research on Adolescence, "Diverging Development: The Not So Invisible Hand of Social Class in the United States." He called on social scientists interested in the study of development to expand their purview beyond investigations of the developmental impacts of poverty and consider the full gamut of social class variation in our increasingly unequal society. The gradations of class alter the social supports, resources, and opportunities, as well as the constraints, facing parents as they attempt to guide their children toward the acquisition of adult roles. This volume examines the impacts of social class origin on the highly formative period of transition to adulthood. Drawing on findings from the Youth Development Study and other sources, the authors examine social class differences in adult child–parent relationships, intimacy and family formation, attainment of higher education, the school-to-work transition, the emergence of work-family conflict, and harassment in the workplace. The authors indicate new directions for research that will contribute to understanding the problems facing young people today. These chapters will persuade those making social policy to develop social interventions that will level the playing field and increase the opportunities for disadvantaged youth to become healthy and productive adults.
ISBN 978-04702-93621

CAD 115 *Conventionality in Cognitive Development: How Children Acquire Shared Representations in Language, Thought, and Action*
Chuck W. Kalish, Mark A. Sabbagh, Editors
An important part of cognitive development is coming to think in culturally normative ways. Children learn the right names for objects, proper functions for tools, appropriate ways to categorize, and the rules for games. In each of these cases, what makes a given practice normative is not naturally given. There is not necessarily any objectively better or worse way to do any of these things. Instead, what makes them correct is that people agree on how they should be done, and each of these practices therefore has an important conventional basis. The chapters in this volume highlight the fact that successful participation in practices of language, cognition, and play depends on children's ability to acquire representations that other members of their social worlds share. Each of these domains poses problems of identifying normative standards and achieving coordination across agents. This volume brings together scholars from diverse areas in cognitive development to consider the psychological mechanisms supporting the use and acquisition of conventional knowledge.
ISBN 978-07879-96970

CAD 114 *Respect and Disrespect: Cultural and Developmental Origins*
David W. Schwalb, Barbara J. Schwalb, Editors
Respect enables children and teenagers to value other people, institutions, traditions, and themselves. Disrespect is the agent that dissolves positive relationships and fosters hostile and cynical relationships. Unfortunately, parents, educators, children, and adolescents in many societies note with alarm a growing problem of disrespect and a decline in respect for self and others. Is this disturbing trend a worldwide problem? To answer this question, we must begin to study the developmental and cultural origins of respect and disrespect. Five research teams report that respect and disrespect are influenced by experiences in the family, school, community, and, most importantly, the broader cultural setting. The chapters introduce a new topic area for mainstream developmental sciences that is relevant to the interests of scholars, educators, practitioners, and policymakers.
ISBN 978-07879-95584

CAD 113 *The Modernization of Youth Transitions in Europe*
Manuela du Bois-Reymond, Lynne Chisholm, Editors
This compelling volume focuses on what it is like to be young in the rapidly changing, enormously diverse world region that is early 21st century Europe. Designed for a North American readership interested in youth and young adulthood, *The Modernization of Youth Transitions in Europe* provides a rich fund of theoretical insight and empirical evidence about the implications of contemporary modernization processes for young people living, learning, and working across Europe. Chapters have been specially written for this volume by well-known youth sociologists; they cover a wide range of themes against a shared background of the reshaping of the life course and its constituent phases toward greater openness and contigency. New modes of learning accompany complex routes into employment and career under rapidly changing labor market conditions and occupational profiles, while at the same time new family and lifestyle forms are developing alongside greater intergenerational responsibilities in the face of the retreat of the modern welfare state. The complex patterns of change for today's young Europeans are set into a broader framework that analyzes the emergence and character of European youth research and youth policy in recent years.
ISBN 978-07879-88890

NEW DIRECTIONS FOR CHILD & ADOLESCENT DEVELOPMENT

ORDER FORM SUBSCRIPTION AND SINGLE ISSUES

DISCOUNTED BACK ISSUES:

Use this form to receive 20% off all back issues of *New Directions for Child & Adolescent Development*.
All single issues priced at **$23.20** (normally $29.00)

TITLE	ISSUE NO.	ISBN
_____	_____	_____
_____	_____	_____
_____	_____	_____

*Call 888-378-2537 or see mailing instructions below. When calling, mention the promotional code JB9ND
to receive your discount. For a complete list of issues, please visit www.josseybass.com/go/ndcad*

SUBSCRIPTIONS: (1 YEAR, 4 ISSUES)

☐ New Order   ☐ Renewal

U.S.	☐ Individual: $85	☐ Institutional: $280
CANADA/MEXICO	☐ Individual: $85	☐ Institutional: $320
ALL OTHERS	☐ Individual: $109	☐ Institutional: $354

*Call 888-378-2537 or see mailing and pricing instructions below.
Online subscriptions are available at www.interscience.wiley.com*

ORDER TOTALS:

Issue / Subscription Amount: $ _____

Shipping Amount: $ _____
(for single issues only – subscription prices include shipping)

Total Amount: $ _____

SHIPPING CHARGES:

SURFACE	DOMESTIC	CANADIAN
First Item	$5.00	$6.00
Each Add'l Item	$3.00	$1.50

*(No sales tax for U.S. subscriptions. Canadian residents, add GST for subscription orders. Individual rate subscriptions must
be paid by personal check or credit card. Individual rate subscriptions may not be resold as library copies.)*

BILLING & SHIPPING INFORMATION:

☐ **PAYMENT ENCLOSED:** *(U.S. check or money order only. All payments must be in U.S. dollars.)*

☐ **CREDIT CARD:** ☐ VISA   ☐ MC   ☐ AMEX

Card number _____ Exp. Date _____

Card Holder Name_____ Card Issue # _____

Signature _____ Day Phone _____

☐ **BILL ME:** *(U.S. institutional orders only. Purchase order required.)*

Purchase order # _____
Federal Tax ID 13559302 • GST 89102-8052

Name_____

Address_____

Phone_____ E-mail_____

Copy or detach page and send to: **John Wiley & Sons, PTSC, 5th Floor
989 Market Street, San Francisco, CA 94103-1741**

Order Form can also be faxed to: **888-481-2665**

PROMO JB9ND

NEW DIRECTIONS FOR
CHILD AND ADOLESCENT DEVELOPMENT
IS NOW AVAILABLE ONLINE AT WILEY INTERSCIENCE

What is Wiley InterScience?

Wiley InterScience is the dynamic online content service from John Wiley & Sons delivering the full text of over 300 leading scientific, technical, medical, and professional journals, plus major reference works, the acclaimed Current Protocols laboratory manuals, and even the full text of select Wiley print books online.

What are some special features of Wiley InterScience?

Wiley Interscience Alerts is a service that delivers table of contents via e-mail for any journal available on Wiley InterScience as soon as a new issue is published online.
EarlyView is Wiley's exclusive service presenting individual articles online as soon as they are ready, even before the release of the compiled print issue. These articles are complete, peer-reviewed, and citable.
CrossRef is the innovative multi-publisher reference linking system enabling readers to move seamlessly from a reference in a journal article to the cited publication, typically located on a different server and published by a different publisher.

How can I access Wiley InterScience?

Visit http://www.interscience.wiley.com.

Guest Users can browse Wiley InterScience for unrestricted access to journal tables of contents and article abstracts, or use the powerful search engine.
Registered Users are provided with a *Personal Home Page* to store and manage customized alerts, searches, and links to favorite journals and articles. Additionally, Registered Users can view free online sample issues and preview selected material from major reference works.
Licensed Customers are entitled to access full-text journal articles in PDF, with select journals also offering full-text HTML.

How do I become an Authorized User?

Authorized Users are individuals authorized by a paying Customer to have access to the journals in Wiley InterScience. For example, a university that subscribes to Wiley journals is considered to be the Customer.
Faculty, staff, and students authorized by the university to have access to those journals in Wiley InterScience are Authorized Users. Users should contact their library for information on which Wiley journals they have access to in Wiley InterScience.

ASK YOUR INSTITUTION ABOUT WILEY INTERSCIENCE TODAY!